WHAT OTHERS ARE SAYING ABOUT THIS BOOK!

"This collection of essays will bless, challenge, and enlighten the reader. The Bible is the most valuable tool one could ever expose themselves too and these essays will help to develop men into the kind of Disciples with which God would be pleased. I'm very excited about project!"

Dr. Henry P. Davis III, Senior Pastor
First Baptist Church of Highland Park
Landover, Maryland

"There are subjects that are in vogue and that represent the 'trend' of the times. There are other subjects that are consistent and, in some ways, eternal and one of them is, what is the intersection between faith and everyday life and how does the Bible impact my life and living. This marvelous book, edited by Dr. Darryl Sims and written by several scholars and practitioners is a God send and a must read. I am excited about this work and highly recommend it."

Bishop Timothy J. Clarke, Senior Pastor
First Church
Columbus, Ohio

"Dr. Darryl D. Sims, along with the other contributors, presents a compelling argument on the ever-evolving topic of Christian Manhood that every man needs to read. This collection of essays will change your life. The interactive questions at the end of each essay are truly an innovative way to engage the men via a weekly group as well as in a monthly gathering. This book is also designed for an individual to read while at home or work. I strongly suggest, you get this book into the hands of every man you know and every man you want to see grow in the Lord. Buy a copy and send it to a friend."

Dr. Clifford Ashe, III
Founder and President of MVM,
Mighty Men of Valor

"This is a rare find! Darryl Sims has put together a treasure trove of practical wisdom and essential resources that will equip Men of all generations and nationalities to live more courageously as authentic Brothers who deeply love God, themselves, their families, and their communities."

Dr. D. Darrell Griffin, Senior Pastor
Oakdale Covenant Church
Chicago, Illinois

"In an era in which manhood is being reconsidered and redefined, Dr. Darryl Sims has provided a thoughtful, spiritually enriching, and practical guide for contemporary Christian Black men. This resource will prove to be critical in the intellectual and spiritual formation of those engaged in the work of ministering to men individually or leading Men's Ministries in congregations. This book reminds us that the Scriptures must be central in the cultivation of healthy expressions of manhood. May we never forget the lessons of this book!"

Dr. Daniel Corrie Schull, Senior Pastor
Burnett Avenue Baptist Church
Louisville, Kentucky

"As a man and pastor who has endured life transitions, embracing my vulnerability has enabled me to grow. My Bible and My Manhood is a collection of transparent essays by men to help men appreciate the inherent value of vulnerability. If you're a man authentically seeking transformation, then My Bible and My Manhood is must have resource!"

Dr. Donald D. Moore, Senior Pastor
Mount Carmel Baptist Church
Philadelphia, Pennsylvania

"My Bible My Manhood is a book every person should read to gain an enhanced consideration of God as it relates to God's expectations of men. This book will challenge you as well as enlighten you in a fresh and formidable way. It will help you realign your walk with God, your conversation with others, and your personal perception of both your failures and triumphs as a man. It is a must read for anyone who desires to improve their relationship with God, self, and others."

Rev. Courtenay L. Miller, Senior Pastor
Norbeck Community Church
Silver Spring, MD
Third District, Chaplain
Omega Psi Phi Fraternity, Inc.

My Bible

My Manhood

BLENDING SPIRITUAL WISDOM AND PRACTICAL
FAITH WITHIN A BROTHER'S DAILY LIVING

WRITTEN BY
10 PROGRESSIVE FAITH
DEVELOPMENT LEADERS

INCLUDES EXTENSIVE INTERACTIVE STUDY GUIDE

EDITED BY DARRYL D. SIMS, Ph.D.
FOREWORD BY DR. FREDERICK D. HAYNES, III

Published by Sims Publishing Group, LLC   Washington, DC 20003

www.simspublishinggroup.com

My Bible My Manhood

Library of Congress Cataloging-in-Publication Data

My Bible My Manhood

Sims, Darryl D.

p. cm

ISBN 978-1-939774-71-2 (pbk. :alk. Paper)

African American faith development. 2. African American socialization. African American male biblical enlighment.

Printed in the United States of America

DEDICATION

I'd like to dedicate this book to mom (Vivian Brown), my dad (Stanford Sims, Jr.), and my three daughters—Darnisha Sims, Latecia Sims-Mix, and Riele Sims. It's with all the joy in the Lord that I dedicate and thank all five of you for helping, lifting, guiding, forgiving, and loving me.

ACKNOWLEDGEMENT

First, I must acknowledge all the contributors for simply participating in the project. Each of them toiled and wrestled with their respective selected passage of scripture. Without being willing to submit to the Holy Spirit I'm not sure how things would've turned out. Next, I want to multiple editors and readers who helped guide this project to its completion. Lastly, I'd like to acknowledge my graphic designer from Starvin Artist who designed the book cover. As well as his administrative genius Jalisa.

TABLE OF CONTENTS

FOREWORD

In the 19th century when British missionaries arrived in the Caribbean with the objective of evangelizing enslaved Africans, they came armed with a heavily edited Bible. Scriptural passages that may have incited rebellion and resistance on the part of the oppressed were extracted. It's been estimated that 90% of the Hebrew Bible, or the First Testament, was cut out of what came to be known as the *Slave Bible*. Over half of the New Testament was removed from its pages. Scriptures that illustrated the liberating power moves of God on behalf of the enslaved were torn from the pages of "The Word of God." All references to justice for the poor and freedom for the oppressed are missing from this "sacred book." One can scour the pages of the *Slave Bible* and not find the inaugural sermon and mission statement of Jesus found in Luke 4:18-19. Jesus declaring "And you shall know the truth and the truth will set you free" in John's gospel is noticeably absent. The enslaved Africans who were taught to read the *Slave Bible* never read about the emancipating Exodus experienced by the enslaved in Egypt or the pronouncements of judgment from the prophets on nations that did not practice justice. The *Slave Bible* was weaponized by the empire in their mission of oppression. Passages that emphasized the responsibility of slaves to their masters were highlighted, taught, and preached. The goal of this "bible" was to produce docile and well-behaved slaves that conformed to systems of oppression and a second-class existence.

Today, just three copies of the *Slave Bible* are known to exist. Two are held in the United Kingdom and one in the United States that is the property of Fisk University. It has been borrowed by the Museum of the Bible in Washington, D. C. in collaboration with the Center for the Study of African American Religious Life at the Smithsonian National Museum of African American History and Culture, according to a report by Michel Martin for NPR.

The *Slave Bible* was diabolically "constructed" to maintain the status quo of racial oppression and colonization. This "bible" was the evil editing of those determined to misuse the power and authority of the "good book" to justify the abuse and othering of the oppressed. The message from the pages of "holy writ" was twisted and distorted to support a political and economic agenda whose vicious vestiges haunt us today.

Modern 21st century humans would be quick to view the *Slave Bible* and be appalled while denouncing it as wicked and wrong; however, a slave bible hermeneutic continues to haunt and harm many as it baptizes patriarchy and defines masculinity through a white male gaze. To remix the language of W. E. B. DuBois: A slave bible hermeneutic is the continued interpretation of the Bible in ways that compromise human freedom, cooperate with injustice, and anoint oppression in its' multiple and varied forms. A slave bible hermeneutic recklessly applies ancient behaviors and models to current practices without an awareness of the historical context of the scriptures or a consciousness of the unjust systems, complexities and evolving attitudes pertaining to gender. Preachers and teachers of the Christian Bible, quick to declare in some traditions, as they hold up the Holy Book, "God said it, I believe it, and that settles it," often interpret the Bible literally through western eyes while ignoring or being ignorant of the latest biblical scholarship that expands our understanding of the world of the Bible, its literary constructs, and the original audience being addressed.

With the gift of hindsight, I can recall an experience with a slave bible hermeneutic practiced by a noted preacher. I was introduced in the early days of my ministry to a popular and revered Southern Baptist preacher after I had addressed a state evangelism conference in the Southern Baptist denomination. After the gracious introduction on my behalf to the evangelical legend, he responded by saying to me, "Always remember, there are many applications of the Word, but only ONE interpretation." I quickly responded, "And who decides what the ONE interpretation is?" Unfortunately, he walked off, refusing to engage in dialogue and exploration of the meaning of his statement; evidently unwilling to grapple with the dangerousness of his declaration. His comment had in its' "DNA" the slave bible hermeneutic, dripping in authoritative literalism. It wasn't lost on me that he was a legend in a denomination that was born out of dissent, divorcing itself from northern Baptists, with the enslavement of Black bodies as the cause for irreconcilable differences. Neither did it go unnoticed that he was conspicuously silent as the Black church based civil rights movement became a revival that set the stage for the United States to experience a Second Reconstruction.

One can conclude that if a book entitled, *My Bible My Manhood* had been written in the 19th century with the *Slave Bible* as the source, the results would have been dehumanizingly harmful, especially to enslaved Black people. Accordingly, if one interprets the "Word of God" through a *Slave Bible* construct today, Christianity remains a weapon for oppression while anointing patriarchy in the name of Jesus and becoming irrelevant (specific to this book) to the intersections of what it means to be a man in the 21st century.

Darryl Sims has gifted to men, many who may have been unknowingly influenced or turned off by the slave bible hermeneutic, a helpful and insightful treatment of the Bible and Manhood. He has assembled a panel of thoughtful and progressive faith leaders who have deeply studied and wrestled with the meaning of sacred scriptures and manhood in a way that is healing, liberating, and empowering. In these pages brothers are invited to interrogate ourselves meditatively through illuminating insights that reflect biblical scholarship, spiritual commitment, and faith-filled wisdom. Like Jacob wrestling with the angel, this book won't easily let the reader go without bequeathing a blessing. The relevance of the material reflects a consciousness of the complexities and intersectionalities that constitute manhood in a complex world. Brothers are invited to feel, think, reflect, and face ourselves in this invitation to wholeness. It invites us to see manhood through an enlightened encounter with God's Word. The structure of the book provides opportunities for one to read and practically apply the healing, liberating and empowering content the panel of sages and seers have carefully and prayerfully written. A thoughtful and prayerful reading of this book will produce a brother who deepens his love for God, himself, and his ability to healthily love and relate to others.

My Bible My Manhood is the fruit of a mission that Darryl Sims has boldly and brilliantly embraced. I have often referred to him as the "Modern Day Apostle Paul," applauding him for his commitment to interpreting and spreading the Gospel through writing. He has often been used in ministry to address the plight of men in general, and Black men particularly. This book reflects the ripe harvest of years of listening to, laboring with and ministering to a demographic that has been criminalized, overpoliced, stereotyped, and misinterpreted while slowly exiting from the pews and ministries of churches throughout the country. Sims has labored among brothers and has sat where they sat, and the result is this game changing powerful work.

An elder in a church where I was privileged to preach shared with me an old Bible that belonged to her father. When she opened the Bible, his identification card fell out. I picked it up and handed it to her. She thanked me and replied, "I forgot that daddy always kept his I. D. in the Word." She smiled and said, "That'll preach, Rev! That's who he was: a good man who got who he was from the Word." *My Bible My Manhood* is destined to challenge us to become good men who understand who we are because of God's Word.

Frederick Douglass Haynes, III
Senior Pastor
Friendship-West Baptist Church
Dallas, TX

PREFACE

Self-paced Individual Study or Interactive Group Discovery and Discussion

The Bible is the greatest resource and tool available to strengthen and encourage us as men. The principles and truths in the Bible can be applied to all life's situations and challenges. *My Bible My Manhood* is designed to disrupt the fallacy that, as men, we must have it all together all the time.

If we're being honest, as men we are uncomfortable showing our emotions and being vulnerable. Point blank. Period. And to go one step further, the pandemic, the social and racial injustices, and overall global unrest have caused "dis-ease" for many. It is increasingly more difficult to manage life's stresses without the tools and resources that offer guidance or encouragement on how to navigate them. We need a safe space to reflect, release, and relate.

The impenetrable walls we've built can be dismantled to create a spirit of transparency and authenticity that does not diminish who we are as men. Being honest with our feelings is not a sign of weakness or fragility. This book is a compilation of essays penned by today's leading voices in ministry, retelling how they journeyed through trials to triumph as men. These personal and raw accounts are meant to create an atmosphere of encouragement and enlightenment.

While each book in this series can be a powerful resource for self-paced study and exploration, the thought-provoking content and commentaries can also be used for in-depth group discovery and discussion, fostering great exchanges and connections among men built on trust.

The essays are not sequential, so you don't have to read them in order. It's okay to read them as you're led. If you're experiencing a challenge or see a topic that immediately resonates with you – you can go directly to it. And if in a group setting, the group can agree upon the order they'd like to follow.

Whether in individual or group study, this safe space approach allows men to feel comfortable removing their masks as they learn Godly truths about their power as sons of God and their purpose as servants of God.

If you are a woman reading this book and are seeking insights into some of the challenges that men experience, this book will help you understand how we may think and express our emotions. Most importantly, if you want to help your man be a better mate, friend, father, lover, and communicator this book is for you.

This book is designed to foster breakthroughs. I sincerely pray that you find the experiences shared enlightening and encouraging as you continue to go and grow with God.

Rev. Darryl D. Sims, Ph.D.

INTRODUCTION

What does it mean to be a man? How is manhood displayed? If you ask one hundred men to describe manhood you will receive an array of answers. Many men within our society cannot articulate what a man is. If one can't state, how can one be it? I will concede that there are multiple perspectives of manhood. How does the church express their meaning of manhood? Why are so many men turned off by the church? Why are so many of our churches led by men but filled with women? What does the bible teach about manhood?

My Bible My Manhood addresses some of the problems that we, as men face. This book provides biblical teaching that speaks directly to many of the questions pertaining to manhood. It will help you understand what it means to be a husband, a mate, a father, a friend, a mentor, and a mature man. You will read personal accounts of bouncing back from a messy and public mistake, preparing someone for your mantle, living a life of morality, experiencing a personal metamorphosis, and excelling in your ministry.

God has blessed me to write numerous books regarding men and men's ministry. While attending Howard University School of Divinity from 1996 to 1999, as an associate minister at the Historic Metropolitan Baptist Church in Washington DC, I was placed over a weekly men's bible study class by the Assistant Pastor, Dr. Keith Kitchen. When I served as the Minister of Men and Evangelism from 1999 to 2002 under the tutelage of Dr. Charles E. Booth at the Mount Olivet Baptist Church, my first book pertaining to the development of men was published by a national mainstream publishing company. In the capacity of the National Coordinator of Urban Ministries, Inc., from 2005 to 2008, my chief responsibility was to travel the country meeting with pastors, ministerial staff, and lay leaders to understand what churches and their members sought regarding support and resources. In each context, there was and remains a need for material that speaks to past and present trauma associated with men. I've discovered that some ministries address the physical needs of men by giving them activities and outreach opportunities. While other ministries address the spiritual formation and expectations of men. And finally, only a handful of teachers and preachers connect and engage with men on all aspects of man.

There is no question that most of our churches offer men spiritual support and resources. However, some men desire more from our churches and church leaders. Men need a deeper level of support and connection. We need safe spaces to admit that we may be struggling in certain areas, we don't have it all together, or we have made costly mistakes that we haven't recovered from. Whatever the struggle, men - it is ok to say you need help and seek spiritual direction and clarity.

To fill this supportive void, God placed on my heart to create this book series compiling the voices, testimonies, and perspectives of men across the globe of varying nationalities and backgrounds. Men who, in full transparency, went through something and are still here to share their stories of reflection, repentance, release, and restoration as they sought direction from God's Word and Way.

We, as men, must rewrite the narrative of what it means to be a man in love with God. We can't allow anyone to take away the beauty of being a child of God. As men, we must acknowledge the connection to one another and value women's contributions and equality. As men, we must acknowledge the Word of God in Genesis 1:26-27 and walk in the truth that men and women are created equally. As well as so much of our success as men have always been and will always be inextricably tied to the women in our lives. Biblical manhood dictates we love the women in our lives as Christ loves the church.

This book series will challenge you and your biblical understanding of being a God-fearing, Bible-reading, and community-loving man. As you read this entire book individually or take the journey through group study, I pray that you will see yourself and God differently and that your relationship with Him and others deepens in forgiveness, love, and peace.

How to Maximize this Book

The essays and lessons shared in this first volume reflect the voices of a diverse group of contributors whose collective transparency are meant to transform your life. The authors provide solid biblical foundational realities of men who wrestled with life's daily challenges. These writers stretched themselves to encourage and stretch you. Each topic presented is organized to take the reader on a journey of enlightenment through the author's commentaries, followed by a study section with questions and exercises to spark reflection and introspection.

After the topic is introduced with a title, definition, and quote, the author's essay is broken down into the following essential components:

- **The Circumstance**: describes the condition or experience faced or encountered along with a Biblical example offering real-life application or action.

- **The Conflict**: presents the clash between the author and the Holy Spirit when attempting to navigate the circumstance.

- **The Choice**: describes the decision to resolve the conflict and address the circumstance.

- **The Consequence**: reveals the outcome or result of the choice that was made.

- **The Challenge**: presents the continued struggle the author experienced in navigating the circumstance.

- **The Christological Principle**: offers a Biblical principle or doctrine of Christ that the author believes aligns with how to address the circumstance effectively.

- **The Crisis:** describes the pivotal turning point for the author as he moved beyond the choice and consequences and sought God for guidance.

- **The Covenant:** A binding agreement made by two or more persons or parties; compact.

- **The Conclusion:** provides a closing summation or thought for you to consider as you read and gain insights and Biblical principles that you can apply to your own life when faced with a similar situation or experience.

Each author's commentary is followed by an opportunity for you to either reflect and study on your own and at your own pace or to discuss in a group setting.

The self-paced format is easy to follow:

- **Five Key Scriptures** are provided that apply to the topic for you to pray about and hold onto so you can apply in your life when faced with a similar situation.

- **Deeper Dive** present questions for introspection and self-reflection. In a group study, share what you are led to. This is a moment to get real with yourself and with God.

- **Application**: offers steps that you can take to carry out what was shared in the "Conclusion" section.

- **Affirmation**: provides a positive word or phrase you can carry with you. You are encouraged to write the affirmation and make it your own, so it becomes more personal for you.

- **Supplication**: offers a brief prayer for you to say aloud.

Invitation: offers an opportunity for you to know Christ and accept Him as your Lord and Savior if you don't have a relationship with Him.

MY BIBLE AND MY MISTAKE:

The Wrong Place, the Wrong Pursuit, and the Wrong Person!

Darryl D. Sims, Ph.D.

Definition:

Mistake: An error or fault; a misconception or misunderstanding.

Quote:

> *"Every man got a right to make his own mistakes.*
> *Ain't no man that ain't made any."*
> — Boxing Champion Joe Louis (1914-1981)

Scripture:

In the spring, at the time when kings go off to war, David sent Joab out with the king's men and the whole Israelite army. They destroyed the Ammonites and besieged Rabbah. But David remained in Jerusalem. One evening David got up from his bed and walked around on the roof of the palace. From the roof he saw a woman bathing. The woman was very beautiful, and David sent someone to find out about her. The man said, "She is Bathsheba, the daughter of Eliam and the wife of Uriah the Hittite." Then David sent messengers to get her. She came to him, and he slept with her. (Now she was purifying herself from her monthly uncleanness.) Then she went back home. The woman conceived and sent word to David, saying, "I am pregnant." So David sent this word to Joab: "Send me Uriah the Hittite." And Joab sent him to David. When Uriah came to him, David asked him how Joab was, how the soldiers were and how the war was going. Then David said to Uriah, "Go down to your house and wash your feet." So Uriah left the palace, and a gift from the king was sent after him. But Uriah slept at the entrance to the palace with all his master's servants and did not go down to his house. David was told, "Uriah did not go home." So he asked Uriah, "Haven't you just come from a military campaign? Why didn't you go home?" Uriah said to David, "The ark and Israel and Judah are staying in tents,[a] and my commander Joab and my lord's men are camped in the open country. How could I go to my house to eat and drink and make love to my wife? As surely as you live, I will not do such a thing!" Then David said to him, "Stay here one more day, and tomorrow I will send you back." So Uriah remained in Jerusalem that day and the next. At David's invitation, he ate and drank with him, and David made him drunk. But in the evening Uriah went out to sleep on his mat among his master's servants; he did not go home. In the morning David wrote a letter to Joab and sent it with Uriah. In it he wrote, "Put Uriah out in front where the fighting is fiercest. Then withdraw from him so he will be struck down and die." (2 Samuel 11: 1-15)

CIRCUMSTANCE

All too often men seek to acquire the things that may look good to them while knowing all along that what or who they are seeking may very well be bad for them. The Bible, in 2 Samuel 11: 1-15, relates an instance wherein it is springtime and King David ought to be at war with his men. The king disobeys ancient kingly protocol, however, and opts to stay home. This decision creates an opportunity for trouble to invade his life. When a man is in the *wrong place*, he can expect trouble to greet him there.

Instead of going off to fight with his men, David elects to stay behind. This decision creates the opportunity for him to go after the *wrong pursuit*—a beautiful woman. She caught David's eye while bathing and he impulsively decides he wants to sleep with her. The Bible teaches us that sin often starts with our eyes, slipping into our thinking, before revealing itself in our actions. That being true in this case, David makes a few inquiries about the woman's identity and her status. He is informed she is Bathsheba, the wife of Uriah—one of his dedicated soldiers. Despite her marital status he sends for her and orders her to sleep with him. Later, after the act of adultery is committed, she realizes that she is pregnant with his child and sends word to David.

David responds by attempting to cover his sin. He summons Uriah, back to Jerusalem from the field of war, hoping that Uriah would sleep with her upon his return and thus assume responsibility for her pregnancy. Devoted to the causes of his God, his king and his country, Uriah refuses to sleep with his wife while his men are on the bloody battlefield. David then implements a different plan and commits yet another sin: the sin of murder as he conspires to have Uriah assigned to the frontlines of a dangerous battle, knowing he wouldn't survive.

The text in this chapter of the Bible reveals the progressive nature of sin, showing that there is always a larger price to be paid for our sinful mistakes after we make the down payment on our choice of sin. Of all the people of Israel, King David, and the man after God's own heart, should have fully understood the difference between a sinful man and a virtuous one of valor, especially during a time of war. When the priest Ahimelech asked about the purity of his men, in 1 Samuel 21:5, David expressly stated: "My men do not sleep with their women during war." David miscalculated the faithfulness and discipline of Uriah to uphold the teachings that David had passed down to his soldiers. So much for the excuse frequently heard among church congregations today: "If Pastor does it, so can I."

David has Uriah deliver his own death notice to Joab, the battlefield commander—a notice directing Joab to place Uriah on the frontline of the battlefield. Thus, David adds another unknowing person to his web of deceit by directing Joab to carry out an order resulting in the death of a loyal soldier. This act reveals how our mistakes affect and infect others as well as ourselves. David was in the *wrong place*. He lusted after the wrong person. His selfish *wrong pursuit* led to deadly results.

CONFLICT

When a man decides to go against what is right, that decision will always lead to something wrong. Mistakes are common to all men, but some mistakes can be overt and intentional. David knew that God expected him to lead the people of Israel by His statutes and by example. He knew that God had anointed him to safeguard the people and not exploit them. He knew that God expected him to rule the people with love and to seek justice for all in the process. David also knew the Torah well, and he knew that God is a God both of love and mercy as well as judgment and wrath. Yet, he allowed the protrusion between his legs to lead him into an act of adultery.

All too often our fellow Christians, the people in our churches today, take advantage of others. This happens on multiple levels. Many take advantage of their positions and influence by demanding to have their way. David, in his position as King of Israel, felt a sense of entitlement that went beyond the rights and privileges ordained to him by God. He placed his throne over the throne of God. He was very much aware of the Ten Commandments, and he knew that he was not to covet another man's wife, commit adultery, or murder anyone. David also was aware that it was he who had demanded sexual abstinence of all the soldiers of Israel involved in war. And he was aware of the Lord's expectation that he would rule the people of Israel in keeping with His directives.

Notwithstanding, David, like many of us, was a master at displaying the dual nature of man that God both loves and despises. Remember, this was the same David who danced in jubilation when the Ark of the Covenant was brought to Jerusalem. This was the same David who refused to kill Saul because of the anointing placed on Saul by God. This was the same David who loved another man, Jonathan, like he had loved no woman. David knew the importance of covenant relationships; still, he goes against the will, the way, and the word of God.

Is it not ironic that a man can focus on something or someone to the point that he refuses to think past the immediate moment or weigh the cost of attaining his heart's desire? Is it also not sad when a man chooses to operate more in the basest realm of his existence—namely, that beneath his waistline—rather than focusing on the spiritual bliss and intimacy extended to him via the God-given privilege of free will to love His people and obey His Word?

CHOICE

Knowing what he knew, David had to accept his role in the disaster that he created by his lust and self-centeredness and with total disregard for the sanctity of the God-ordained institution of marriage. David had to accept responsibility for this mistake because he was the king. While he could never make things right with all the parties involved, he knew he had to repent and make things right with his relationship with God. This is evident in 2 Samuel when David is later confronted by Nathan the prophet and is forced to look at his mistake and take responsibility for his actions.

Like David, we Christian men of today must own up to our mistakes and be ready to face any backlash that may result. I can testify personally to the internal and external liberation that comes when one owns up to his mistakes and petitions God for forgiveness. The hardest thing to accomplish during this process is forgiving oneself.

I can testify to the burden of being labeled because of my mistakes. I can testify to the hurt of being dropped and dismissed by the very ones I thought would embrace me as a son, a nephew, and a friend in the ministry after my mistake was made public. It is with a deep level of sadness that I must concede that in most situations it is the preacher, having received a triple portion of grace from God and from the people, who is the most judgmental and unforgiving.

When appropriate, it is vital for all men to point the first finger of blame at themselves. As Christian men, we must rise to a new level of accountability and responsibility for our actions. "Because a sermon seen is more effective than a sermon heard," as the great poet, Langston Hughes advised. And biblically speaking, the Lord requires us to be walking epistles. I once left a church because of the damage my actions caused within it and the church community. To clarify, I did not actually leave the church; rather, I left my God-ordained post, and in essence, I left God. Or so I thought because God did not leave me. The bible teaches, where can we go, and God not already be there? Now I truly understand that my first level of accountability was to God and not to the church. And not to my selfish and self-centered longings.

Returning to the text, after a conversation with the prophet Nathan, David ultimately took ownership of his misguided desires and complete disregard for the marital covenant between Uriah and Bathsheba. To reiterate, like David, we the men of God must take ownership of our mistakes and, when we do, seek forgiveness for our actions from the people and from our Lord! The choices we make as men should be a direct reflection of our relationship with God.

We must seek to nurture our relationship with God daily. This in turn will assist us in our decision-making processes when confronted with a "Bathsheba Moment." We should not limit such moments merely to those resulting from our misguided attractions to captivating and/or seductive women. Every choice we make that we *know* is outside the will of God and that will lead to personal gain for us while ensuring personal loss for someone else can possibly be viewed as a Bathsheba Moment. All our decisions that are self-serving, self-centered, and selfish can be viewed in the same light. These moments can involve our business dealings, our friendships, or our desires to grow within our social networks. They reflect a flaw in our character development as well as our dysfunctional decision-making skills. David concentrated more on what he was getting and less on what he was sacrificing to acquire it.

My advice: Brothers, please re-calculate your previous calculations of your personal potential Bathsheba Moments. Choose once and choose wisely.

CONSEQUENCE

Many of the choices that men make can lead to the hurt, harm, or even death of a relationship, movement, or person. David's choice led to the death of a marriage, a soldier, and a baby. All too often, we men do not realize until it is too late, or we are too deep into our actions that a very high price is associated with our mistakes and our choices. I know from personal experience that a single decision I made altered my life and delayed my destiny. Like David, I abused my God-ordained position, by sleeping with a married woman and it cost me the divine privilege of pastoring a church. Yet, after I admitted the truth to myself, I realized that it cost me not only my relationship with the people within the church but also with people around the country. It is not the actions of a man that receive the most attention but the character flaws that produced those actions.

One might ask: what was going on with David that he would feel comfortable sleeping with another man's wife? What was going on in my mind that would usher me into a potentially deadly situation with another man? Better question, what leads men to make sinful choices displeasing to God? Taking it to another level, why did David or I not consider the possible damage of our relationships with God as a major factor in our actions? The cost of my choice was more than I could ever have bargained for or assumed I would ever have to pay. Now I know that before one acts in an irresponsible manner, one must first think about the potential loss of favor from God, trust from friends, as well as the hurt those actions may cause in one's community. In my case, an entire church community.

Corrupt choices always lead to costly casualties. Therefore, choose wisely. The mistakes you make outside of God's will, way, or word can alter your life and impede your potential.

CHALLENGE

I am aware of the many struggles that we as men face with our sexual inclinations and selfish desires. It is a struggle for many men—from the pulpit to the pew and from the boardroom to the basketball court. There are times when it is simply difficult to stay obedient to the Word of God, in general; but for many men, it appears to be an extremely difficult struggle to control one's zipper.

Our challenge as men goes beyond race and religion. The challenge is to eliminate the mentality of male entitlement. Like David, many contemporary men have taken on a spirit of insatiable greed, and it is more than a Black, Latino, Asian, or White thing—it is a male thing. The moral decay of America is truly one of several factors that play into the dangerous level of comfort many men today have with committing blatant acts of sin. Many men have become too familiar with the supremacy and sovereignty of God. Such perspectives contradict biblical teachings referencing of the reverence of God. Men must decide who and what will control their minds, feelings, and actions. About this, the Bible is clear: "But seek ye first the kingdom of God, and His righteousness; and all these things shall be added unto you" (Matthew 6:33).

Our challenge as men is to make the right choice—namely, a choice that reflects our love for God. As men, we must choose to be more like God and less like other men. Jesus is the man we should strive to emulate and imitate. We need only to look at His life, personality, and character to receive our manly marching orders. We should follow His earthly examples of manhood and make concerted efforts to be more like Him.

CHRISTOLOGICAL PRINCIPLE

The Bible relates that a group of religious leaders once brought a woman to Jesus for punishment, claiming that they caught the woman in the act of adultery. Jesus instead told the woman her sins were forgiven but to "go and sin no more." The lesson to be learned from this is that the act of adultery is wrong, but the act of forgiveness is right!

CRISIS

Many men never have a chance to display their skills because of a mistake they made in their lives. Many marriages end in divorce court because too many men seek to be pleased rather than to please their wives. Many men find themselves in prison because of a mistake they made in their youth. Many preachers find themselves out of a church because of mistakes they made while not being in alignment with the guiding from the Holy Spirit. Many of the most talented athletes will never play organized sports on any level because of mistakes they made in high school and college. Sadly, the greatest indictment that can be brought against many of the men in many of our churches is our silence. Many do not have a prophet Nathan in their lives like David. They have no other wiser, older man to speak with about their mistakes or to guide them away from sin and toward the fullness of their priestly roles within their families, churches, and communities.

COVENANT

Men who struggle with making godly decisions should seek professional assistance to help them get honest about their proclivities and propensities. It is imperative for churches to cultivate prayer-partner relationships with men who are strong in the areas in which others are weak. All men need an accountability partner in their lives. God can fulfill that role—only to a certain point. Every man should have a peer that he's willing to listen, to learn, and lean from and upon.

CONCLUSION

The primary problem with most men as it relates to making mistakes and committing sin is in our comfortability with God. As men, we must recognize our inability to manipulate God when we find ourselves in the wrong place, with the wrong person, and with our misdirected pursuits. It is vital for all men to deal with their internal struggles and their misguided proclivities. Sin is real. However, forgiveness is available for those of us who are willing to confess our sins and ask God to forgive us. We all miss the mark and fall short as men. Nevertheless, as I once heard Dr. Beecher Hicks, Jr. of Metropolitan Baptist in Washington, DC say during a bible study class, "The goal of all God's people ought never to sin. However, the least we could do is sin less and less as we mature in God's word and love." Brothers, learn to ask for forgiveness for your mistakes and to accept the power of apologizing to those you have harmed.

FIVE KEY SCRIPTURES

1. "Blessed is the man that endureth temptation: for when he is tried, he shall receive the crown of life, which the Lord hath promised to them that love him." (James 1:12)

2. "If we confess our sins, he is faithful and just to forgive us our sins, and to cleans us from unrighteousness. If we say that we have not sinned, we make him a liar, and his word is not in us." (1 John 1:9-10)

3. "Brothers, if someone is caught in a sin, you who are spiritual should restore him gently. But watch yourself, or you also may be tempted." (Galatians 6:1)

4. "The fear of the Lord is the beginning of wisdom: and the knowledge of the holy is understanding." (Proverbs 9:10)

5. "When I was a child, I spake as a child, I understood as a child, I thought as a child: but when I became a man, I put away childish things." (1Corinthians 13:11)

DIVE DEEPER

1. What is the one mistake you made that still haunts you to this day?

2. Who helped you with the process of rebounding and rebuilding from this mistake?

3. What have you learned from your mistake?

4. How did your mistake impact your relationship with God?

5. How is your relationship with God today?

6. How should we as men help other men once they confess their mistakes to us?

7. Can you recall a mistake that someone you know made from which you learned an important lesson?

8. What is the biggest mistake you feel the government has made in your lifetime?

APPLICATION

1. Pray to God daily to help you with your temptations.

2. "Confess your mess" to a trusted friend prior to acting upon your selfish desires.

3. Discuss your temptations with your wife and pray together to overcome them as a couple.

AFFIRMATION

I now know that my past mistakes don't define or diminish my present manhood.

SUPPLICATION

Dear Lord, I seek your healing and forgiveness for all men who have an authentic desire to nurture their relationships with You. Thank you for my personal deliverance from my mistakes. It is this servant's prayer that I and men everywhere will seek to correct and reconcile mistakes and broken relationships. It is my hope that Your love, compassion, and grace will rest within our hearts so we will be better men within our households, communities, and churches. Amen.

INVITATION

I invite you to give Jesus the broken pieces of your life and any unresolved mistakes you may have made. In doing so trust that you'd be made whole. Continue to place your heart, mind, and soul in the hands of God. I encourage you to seek God's will for your life.

MY BIBLE AND MY MATE:

They Shall Be One

Dr. Gary L. Williams Sr.,

**Senior Pastor, First Baptist Church of Mandarin,
Jacksonville FL; President of Mymax Corporation**

Definition:

Mate: The woman to whom a man is married; companion

Quote:

> *"When a match has equal partners then I fear not."*
> — Aeschylus, Greek dramatist (BC 525-BC 45)

Scripture:

"And the Lord God said, It is not good that the man should be alone; I will make him an help meet for him. And out of the ground the Lord God formed every beast of the field, and every fowl of the air; and brought them unto Adam to see what he would call them: and whatsoever Adam called every living creature, that was the name thereof. And Adam gave names to all cattle, and to the fowl of the air, and to every beast of the field; but for Adam there was not found an help meet for him. And the Lord God caused a deep sleep to fall upon Adam, and he slept: and he took one of his ribs and closed up the flesh instead thereof; And the rib, which the Lord God had taken from man, made he a woman, and brought her unto the man. And Adam said, This is now bone of my bones, and flesh of my flesh: she shall be called Woman, because she was taken out of Man. Therefore, shall a man leave his father and his mother, and shall cleave unto his wife: and they shall be one flesh." (Genesis 2:18-24)

CIRCUMSTANCE

Life is based on systems, and systems work in tandem with other structures. Viewed in that light, the Book of Genesis takes its rightful place at the vanguard of all the manuscripts that comprise the scriptural canon. If you think about the various organizations of human life—such as the educational, penal, economic, spiritual, and social systems—they all begin in the Book of Genesis. At the core of all the aforementioned systems, however, is the institution of the family, which

God, in His sovereignty and wisdom, established as essential elements of human existence above and before the systems of government, commerce, and even the church came about. The Almighty was keenly aware that if life, government, and social order were to exist, those entities would need a point of origin. Thus, the family, in accordance with His plan, is the foundation and springboard for all social order.

Although man is capable of making things, creation is reserved exclusively for the Almighty. After crafting the solar system, firmament, animals, vegetation, and the crown of His creation—man—God acknowledged the final component needed for the completion of His creative efforts—woman. As Genesis 2:18 avows: "And the Lord God said, it is not good that the man should be alone: I will make him an help meet for him."

Understanding what God said in this passage is equally as important as comprehending what He did *not* say. The word "meet" is taken from the Hebrew *ezer*, which refers to an aid or helper. Too often men view marriage in a light expecting their wife or wife-to-be to complete them. I'm sure you have heard some men say, "She completes me?" Yet, just as a woman does not complete a man, a man does not complete a woman. Just as Adam was complete prior to God presenting Eve to him, men also are complete prior to their nuptials.

Let's examine Genesis 18:2 further. Notice two things about this verse. First, God is doing all the talking. Next, God is not speaking *to* Adam; He is speaking to Himself *about* Adam. The bottom line is that Adam never said that he was alone, neither did he ask God for a wife. God designed Eve to aid, help, and assist Adam, not to complete him. When God made Adam, he was complete in every way—spiritually, physically, and emotionally. In fact, Adam was so complete, he didn't even know he was alone until God presented Eve to him.

We often hear guys say "I gotta get married soon" or "I need to find me a wife"; or we hear them begging others with "Do you know a woman I can talk to?" The reality, however, is this: before a man can be with a woman, he must first be capable of living with himself! Societies are filled with men who lead scrambled lives and who scramble other folks' lives due to this confusion. The Book of Genesis tells us to the contrary that God brought Eve to Adam because he was settled, sound, saved, and secure. Eve didn't complete Adam, *God did*!

CONFLICT

Genesis 2:24 affirms the following: "Therefore shall a man leave his father and mother, and shall cleave unto his wife, and they shall be one flesh." If this Scripture is true, then why do so many Christians divorce their spouses? Why do scores of Christian men and women, touting "irreconcilable differences," file for annulment from their marriages to their Christian mates? The answer is simple: much of the Christian divorce rate can be attributed to views that differ from those of Scripture.

Note that the latter part of verse 24 empathizes that a man and his wife "shall be *one flesh.*" If, as stated in 2 Timothy 3:16, all Scripture is given by inspiration of God, then it is neither an accident nor a coincidence that God told Adam and Eve that they would become one flesh rather than one spirit. Genesis 2:19-23 reveals the process by which The Almighty brought Adam his wife: first, He put Adam to sleep, then He retrieved a rib from Adam's side to form Eve before bringing her to him. What made Eve suitable for Adam was the fact that she was physically and spiritually compatible with him, having been made *of* him.

The reason so many Christian couples lack oneness is because they come to the table of marriage with only part, half, or none of the equation. Many of today's male-female relationships are often one-sided. While one partner—typically the man—focuses on the physical aspect of the union; the other, the woman usually, focuses on the spiritual. Hence, many relationships lack proper balance. It is and will always be an arduous task to become one with a person who is not balanced. Furthermore, unbalanced people are often considered high maintenance. Having one thing in common will not compensate for having twenty-five things that are different. Just because God fashioned Eve for Adam does not mean a man can fashion a mate for himself. When much of a man's time is spent attempting to transform his mate into something he wants them to be, he is attempting to assume the role of God; however, the oneness envisioned by God must occur naturally. It cannot be forced.

CHOICE

It is God's desire for a man to marry with the intent of becoming one with his wife. Unfortunately, all too often men are culpable of cleaving to surrogates other than their designated help meet. Countless marriages are on the rocks because wives are competing with their husband's mother, career, social life, church, mistress(es), or friends. God's intention, to the contrary, is for men to become one with their mates physically, emotionally, and spiritually.

When a man chooses to settle for a help meet in the biblical sense, he makes a conscious decision to have all his physical needs gratified by that woman; the faith and friendship inherent in his relationship with his wife should be in a class by itself. Too often problems in the home arise when a man connects with other women emotionally or spiritually rather than with his wife. When a man subscribes to God's thought processes, however, the oneness of flesh described in the Bible is enhanced. That process is hindered when men do not adhere to the plan of God.

Part of becoming of one flesh entails two actions: leaving and cleaving. It was never God's aim for a man to marry and live with his parents or in-laws. Notably, the Genesis passages pertaining to marriage focus first on God, then on the wife. Although Adam did not have a mother and father, God's instructions were designed to set a precedence throughout humanity. Leaving the home of his original family (mother and father) infers that a man is both independent and of age to take care of himself and his help meet. It also means that a man must be willing and have the wherewithal to start a new family and sustain a household. At the point of this departure, as per the order of God, a man's parents become his secondary family and his new family (wife and children) becomes his primary family.

It will always be difficult, to say the least, to become one with someone with whom you are neither honest nor compatible. Whenever a man attempts to become one with his wife without making the choice of committing to her, his marriage will be suspect. Surely, matrimony today bears a greater weight than when God created Eve for Adam. The Adam of old only had Eve on which to focus; today's Adam must contend with the distractions of Evelyn, Erica, Elizabeth, and Elaine. Therefore, he must make a conscious choice to safeguard not only his marriage but also his integrity and reputation.

CONSEQUENCE

God made man a free moral agent. Being a free moral agent gives man the right to choose even though consequences accompany every choice a man makes. Despite being able to make his own selections, man is not able to select his own consequences. Whenever a man adheres to the oracles of the Almighty, his obedience brings about God's blessings, yet when a man varies from what the Almighty has ordered for his life, difficulty is often guaranteed.

A man's understanding of the oneness required of a married couple begins with the oneness demonstrated, or not demonstrated, by his parents. Children learn about life first by observing the things that transpire in their home. For example, when I was growing up, whenever old folks did not want us children to pick up their bad habits they would say, "Do as I say, not as I do." Do you think we followed their advice? Absolutely not! We did just as they had done! What the older generations failed to understand was those visual lessons—good, bad, or indifferent—are just as potent, if not more so, as vocal lessons. The young are but a microcosm of the macrocosm created by their parents. A man's understanding of oneness is derived from what he observes of his parents' behaviors and attitudes.

For example, if a boy's mother continually internalizes her feelings while his dad freely speaks whatever comes to his mind, there is a good chance that boy, as a man, will seek out and repeat the same pattern in his married relationship. Dysfunctional parents are often culpable for raising dysfunctional children. For this reason, countless Christian marriages are nothing more than a charade. You would be amazed at the number of Christian couples who lead and are active in their churches, respected by their peers, and have a great reputation on their jobs, yet their home life is a mess. Why? Because no oneness has been established between the husband and his wife. This charade sends the wrong message to the children born of such a union. It sends the message that being successful and respected and presenting a façade of bondedness outside the home is more important than being respected, successful, and of one flesh inside the home.

The lack of oneness between husband and wife has a direct impact on how the children of such unions view male-female relationships. Communication, friendship, trust, confidence, and love are all pillars of a good marriage. All these components are essential for harmony and unity in the home. When these are absent, marriage is reduced to a mere "arrangement" lacking any substance or unity.

CHALLENGE

It is imperative for Christian men to understand that certain prerequisites should be in place prior to them saying "I do." In the beginning, God was an excellent paragon for Adam. The very first glimpse the Bible offers of God is of Him at work. As Genesis 1:1 asserts: "In the beginning God created the heavens and the earth." Genesis 2:5 goes on to announce one of God's purposes for creating man: "…and there was not a man to till the ground." In later verses, Paul's spiritual son in the faith, Timothy, declares: "But if any do not provide nor for his own, and especially for those of his own house, he hath denied the faith, and is worse than an infidel." (1 Timothy 5:8) Thus, the enduring message of Scripture—indeed, the challenge for men for all time—is that they must work!

The Bible challenges men to provide for their families; it is part of their spiritual DNA. God has ordained men as priests, protectors, and providers of the home. Even if a man's spouse earns more than he does, he should still make a substantial contribution to his family. If his home is suffering financial hardship, it behooves him to work a second or even a third job, if necessary. A man's ability to provide for his family not only provides merited respect but also gives his wife much-needed assurance regarding the security and safety of the family.

Men are challenged additionally to understand the worth of their help meets. God took a rib from Adam and created Eve. Adam called her bone of his bone and flesh of his flesh. So, ought men to love their wives as their own bodies? He that loveth his wife loveth himself." (Ephesians 5:29) Eve was a part of Adam, physically, spiritually, and emotionally. Any time a man views his help meets outside of these three dimensions, he ignores important parts of her worth. If a husband is only in tune to his wife emotionally and negates the spiritual and physical sides of her, he is responsible for creating a void in her life. Infidelity often occurs in relationships as a result. As is commonly heard, if a husband fails to communicate with his wife, someone else will.

CHRISTOLOGICAL PRINCIPLE

As Christ is quoted in Matthew 12:25, "Every kingdom divided against itself is brought to desolation; and every city or house divided against itself shall not stand." The welfare of a family, team, group, business, or kingdom rest on unity. The failure of inner unity is a recipe for disaster.

CRISIS

Given that we live today in a time of self-proclaimed prophets and prophetesses, it is imperative that all men should know the Word of God for themselves. For years, Christians have been guilty of crediting God for things God neither approved nor ordained. The world is filled with Christians who contend that God blessed them with a certain house or vehicle even when someone else has moved into their homes or driven off with their cars.

How many times have you heard someone say, "God told me to tell you that you were my husband?" or "God spoke to me and told me that you were to be my wife"? Oftentimes, when these self-proclaimed prophecies do not work out, the pseudo-proclaimers make some spiritual excuse as to why their situations or circumstances did not work out. They choose to "spiritualize" everything, blaming "the devil" for their divorces, failures, problems, and so on. Though the devil's existence cannot be denied, these people typically give him more credit than he deserves. The bottom line is that part of the reason for the high divorce rate among Christian couples is that they should never have come together in the first place!

COVENANT

Just as the Apostle Paul commanded Timothy to commit himself to faithful men, so should you. Association brings assimilation. When one assimilates the lives of people one associates with, one becomes like them. As I often tell my own children, I associate only with people whose morals and values are commensurate with my own. The value of doing this has brought me tremendous dividends. I teach my sons specifically that it is not enough to merely be accountable to God, a man must also be accountable to our Godly brothers. I tell them there is a difference between me holding them accountable and me holding their hands. I tell them: you are a man, so act like one!

CONCLUSION

1. Marriage is sacred to God, and a man should treat it as such.

2. God does not want husbands and wives to merely coexist; He wants them to be one.

3. Oneness entails God choosing a compatible mate for a man.

4. Prior to social order, government, and even the church, God established the institution of family. His purpose for doing so stems from the fact that all these entities originate from the union between a husband and wife. Given that God made the family His top priority, it is only right that we Christians do the same. Therefore, our first ministry is not the church, career, or anything else. Our first priority is our home.

FIVE KEY SCRIPTURES

5. "Wherefore they are no more twain, but one flesh. What therefore God hath joined together, let not man put asunder." (Matthew 19:6)

6. "Can two walk together, except they be agreed?" (Amos 3:3)

7. "For this cause shall a man leave his father and mother, and shall be joined unto his wife, and they two shall be one flesh." (Ephesians 5:31)

8. "What? know ye not that he which is joined to a harlot is one body? for two, saith he, shall be one flesh." (1 Corinthians 6:16 KJV)

9. "Two are better than one; because they have a good reward for their labour." (Ecclesiastes 4:9)

DIVE DEEPER

1. Discuss how a lack of oneness between a wife and husband affects their children.

2. What are your feelings about a man's role as the primary keeper of the home even when his wife is "bringing home the bacon?"

3. Do you think who a man associates with outside of his marriage can affect that marriage for better or for worse? Explain.

4. Do you think it is proper for a man to marry and live with his parents? Explain.

5. What are your feelings about men who marry and are immediately separated from their spouse (i.e., deployment, careers, etc.)?

6. Is it important to be in tune with your spouse emotionally? Explain.

APPLICATION

1. During difficult situations, it is important for you to remember the worth (good) of your help meet. Men often do not think about the good in their spouses when they are focusing on the bad.

2. Wives are not perfect, and neither are their husbands. Just as Adam and Eve made mistakes, you and your wife will do the same. There is a difference between striving for oneness and striving for perfection.

3. Pray and seek the face of God for things you can do to enhance the unity of your marriage/relationship. It is always easier to pick out the faults of others as opposed to your own. Remember that there is always room for improvement.

AFFIRMATION

Lord, you intended marriage to be enjoyable, so I will enjoy my marriage!

SUPPLICATION

Lord, you are the source of my strength and the strength of my life. No one lives a problem-free life, so I am aware that difficulties are imminent; however, I know that with you, through you, and by you, all things are possible to he who believes. I pray for the sanctity of my home, the fidelity of my nuptials, and the peace to support each other. Protect us from outside influences that would attempt to put asunder what You have put together. This petition I offer, in Jesus' name, Amen.

INVITATION

"Jesus came that we might have life and have it more abundantly." (John 10:10) If you open the door of your heart, He is willing to have sweet communion with you. Before you become one with anyone, you must first become one with Christ!

MY BIBLE AND MY MANTLE:

It's On You

Dr. Christopher Michael Jones,

Lead Pastor, First Baptist Church of Hillside, NJ; Adjunct Professor and Co-Mentor of the D.Min. Program in Pastoral Care and Counseling, New Brunswick Theological Seminary

Definition:

Mantle: An outer cloak used for additional covering and warmth, especially at night; a symbol of authority, responsibility, or identity; a metaphor for a spiritual covering.

Quote:

> *"Elisha did not need to invent novelties; desiring to have the aid of the same God, he was content to wear the mantle of his predecessor."*
> — Charles Spurgeon

Scripture:

"So he departed thence, and found Elisha the son of Shaphat, who was plowing with twelve yoke of oxen before him, and he with the twelfth: and Elijah passed by him, and cast his mantle upon him. And he left the oxen, and ran after Elijah, and said, Let me, I pray thee, kiss my father and my mother, and then I will follow thee. And he said unto him, Go back again: for what have I done to thee? And he returned back from him, and took a yoke of oxen, and slew them, and boiled their flesh with the instruments of the oxen, and gave unto the people, and they did eat. Then he arose, and went after Elijah, and ministered unto him." (1 Kings 19:19–21)

CIRCUMSTANCE

One of the most praiseworthy goals a man of faith can ever aspire to accomplish in life is participating in the preparation and empowerment of a rising generation. History teaches that for any vision or historical movement to be successful in the long run, each generation must play its part in preparing the next generation to expand upon the achievements and accomplishments of the previous one. Without exception, the Bible bears witness to the need for a planned transference of spiritual leadership and authority between generations. Beginning with God's mandate for fruitfulness in Genesis 1:28 and 9:1, God made it clear that what He established should be properly maintained between succeeding generations.

The same can be said about prophetic movements orchestrated by the hands of mighty men of God. Men in each generation have a distinct mantle of responsibility to further God's agenda and intended purposes on earth. The word "mantle" in this sense refers to one's spiritual authority or divinely appointed role within a community for the purpose of ensuring that God's created order continues to prosper and flourish according to His word.

The story of Elijah and Elisha in 1 Kings 19:19-21 connotes two potent spiritual truths about the transference of mantles between generations. The first of these is that every man in each generation has something to give. Second, every man in each generation has something to receive. Elijah's story actually begins in 1 Kings 17:1, when the word of God provoked him to become a defender of faith serving the one true God of Israel. Elijah's call to the prophetic ministry propelled him into a cosmic battle with King Ahab and Jezebel. The reason for the battles described in 1 Kings 17-18 pertained to Ahab and Jezebel's persistence in Baal worship and their lack of empathy for God's suffering people. Verse 18 of 1 Kings details how Elijah successfully routed over 450 false Baal prophets and proved, through public demonstration, that Yahweh was/is the true God of Israel.

In 1 Kings 19, however, Elijah's strength begins to wane from the struggle. Carrying the mantle of leadership had become overly burdensome to him, to the point where Elijah wanted to give it away. Verse 4 of that biblical chapter captures a moment when Elijah sat under a bush to contemplate the physical and psychological wear-and-tear associated with carrying the mantle of leadership. All he could muster to say to God was "I have had enough, Lord…. Take my life; I am no better than my ancestors."

Speaking from the perspective of an African American man, I concur that carrying the mantle of leadership is as burdensome for today's godly man as it was for Elijah. Not only are we Christian men engaged in a battle against the Baals of our time, but many of us also struggle to maintain our stamina due to the intensity and complexity of the sociopolitical challenges we currently face. In the eyes of the dominant culture, the Black male represents the most stopped-and-frisked, unlawfully detained, racially profiled, and intellectually inept of all in American society. We are stereotyped as being the most violent, the most derelict, the most unimaginative, the most unpatriotic, and the most politically uneducated. If we are not being blamed for our own apathy on the southside of Chicago, we're being blamed for our lack of social progress in the South Ward of Newark, and all manner of points beyond.

On the surface, it would seem as if today's adult African American male has nothing to give back to the next generation. Taking a superficial look, one could easily conclude that the Black man of

America has lost his way with God. The National Center for Law and Economic Justice suggests that many of today's African American males are so despondent and perpetually gripped with inner despair that we are three times more likely to live in deep poverty and no longer have the strength to fight the trends that speak to our demise. The story of Elisha and Elijah, however, should inspire us to reject such notions and be mindful that the mantle we carry is worth far more than silver and gold. Much like Elijah, not only do we carry the mantle of faith, strength, determination, and, when need be, the righteous indignation of our ancestors, we also carry a prophetic word that says "go back the way you came" (1 Kings 19:15) and finish the work God ordered us to complete. Black man, God's mantle is on you!

As God-fearing men of faith, African American men must be willing to do as 1 Kings 19:19 prescribes: to "throw our cloaks" around our families, our children, and our communities and to lift up our self-esteem, our visions, and our dreams. Like Frederick Douglass, Paul Robeson, Dr. Martin Luther King Jr., and Rev. Al Sharpton, we must be willing to see ourselves as holy men of God who have been given a divine purpose and mission. We carry the mantle of leadership and prophetic discernment that enables us to look beyond the stereotypical images of our portrayal in the media and embrace a more holistic view of ourselves as partners with our women and children in the kingdom of God.

It's time for today's Black man of God to accept the notion that we have been given a biblical mandate to stand tall in the places where there is no hope and provide spiritual direction to and cover for our families. We also must realize that it is time for us to snatch back our young women and men and mentor them as they prepare to partner with God in His redemptive plan of liberation.

CONFLICT

Not only do we African American men have much to give to our young, but our young men also have something that we need to receive from them. Verse 20 of 1 Kings affirms that after Elijah approached Elisha and threw his mantle around Elisha, "Elisha then left his oxen and ran after Elijah....Let me kiss my father and mother goodbye," he said, "and then I will come with you."

I often hear these questions: Can today's young Black male learn anything from the older adult males in his community? Is it possible to establish and maintain a communication bridge between the eight-track, cassette tape, and iPod generation? Are the Black men of today willing to listen to the youth in their community? Has the shift in culture and technology caused too great of chasm to overcome? Are the Elijahs in our Black communities too afraid to make room for the emerging Elishas? To these questions, I often respond with a Ghanaian proverb that says, "No man rules forever on the throne of time." In other words, the Elijah Generation must be intentional about making room for the Elisha Generation.

Verse 19 of 1 Kings offers a wonderful and creative way for the more mature adult males in the Black community to connect with younger males. "So, Elijah went from there and found Elisha son of Shaphat," it begins, adding "He was plowing with twelve yoke of oxen, and he himself was driving the twelfth pair." I take this to mean that rather than demand the younger males in our communities to meet us older Black men at our traditional places of comfort and familiarity, we must go where the young males are gathering and try speaking with them in their own language.

As a former multi-platinum hip-hop and R&B producer, having produced the likes of Nasty Nas, Notorious B.I.G., S.W.V., and Mary J. Blige, I can attest that most of the young adults of today would have never come to know the soulful songs of my generation, from the 1960s and 1970s, without having heard many of the those classics after they were sampled in the hip-hop hits of the 1980s and 1990s. Intergenerational dialogue can only take place in similar fashion, when communal sampling takes place among multiple generations. Many of today's young Black men never may have known what it is like to have a father in the home; but instead of demanding that they, lacking father figures, be accountable to their own families, we older Black men should meet them where they are and go from there. We should be permitted to intertwine our careful thoughts with our younger counterparts, and the younger men should be permitted to intertwine their dreams and visions with us. Black man, God's mantle is on you!

Verse 20 of this potent biblical chapter yields another wonderful insight. It reveals that when Elijah found Elisha and covered him with his mantle, Elisha bestowed upon Elijah the decency to stop what he was doing and met the elder man halfway: "Elisha then left his oxen and ran after Elijah." This implies that Elisha had to give up part of what had become most familiar to him to receive a full portion of what the more experienced Elijah had to offer. This is an important observation younger Black man need to understand. Though it may be the case that 2 Chains, Jay-Z, Drake, and Kanye all speak to an authentic urban experience known to far too many of our young Black males, Marvin Gaye's classic hit "What's Going On?" arguably still offers the best commentary on the social ills of the day. Yes, as stated in verse 21, Elisha did indeed sacrifice his "yoke of oxen" to convey to his community his intention to follow his new master, but the first sacrifice Elisha made in his heart was his willingness to stop what he was doing to embrace a God-moment between himself and Elijah.

It takes courage, and a lot of faith, to admit that you need an Elijah in your life. It takes courage to accept that you need help identifying your greater purpose in the world. It takes courage believe that you cannot set your moral compass by yourself. It also takes a lot of faith to give up part of what has become most familiar to you for the sake of embracing an alternative reality through the mentorship of someone else. The Elishas of today need to learn that although the digitization of life may seem more appropriate in today's iPad- and Android-driven world, much remains to be said about experiencing life through the soulful, textured, and analog interpretative lens of an Elijah.

What do our young Black men receive when they meet the Elijahs in our communities halfway? One could make the case that they receive a double portion of their elders' yoke-breaking strength, wisdom, and faith cultivated through hundreds of years of struggling for justice and equality in America. What do we older Black men receive when we are intentional about seeking relationship with the young or inexperienced Elishas in our community? One could make the case that we receive an enhanced sense of purpose, fulfillment, self-worth, and conviction, knowing that the life experiences we can share with this emerging generation will help prepare them for the challenging road ahead. We also receive a sense of fulfillment in knowing that out of our own obedience to God, the mantle we have been given will continue to work its liberating power through the lives of the younger generation. Black men of God, God's mantle is on *you!*

CHOICE

As the social challenges that disproportionately affect African American males continue to increase in urban communities, it has been become increasingly clear that we need to reclaim our prophetic mantle as faithful men of God to restore hope and prosperity to the places that have become arid and dry. Inner-city Black youth are experiencing alarming high school dropout rates, staggering rates of homicide, and epidemic rates of incarceration. Gun violence is destroying our youth like never before while the escalating jobless rate is killing off the hopes of those who have not fallen victim to firearms. To be sure, many organizations across the United States and abroad have developed mentoring programs to provide greater support to Black youth, and especially young Black men. All sorts of one-on-one, school-based, career-based, group-mentoring, and internet-mentoring programs have been created, each seeking to find new ways to empower our young men and women. For example, President Barack Obama launched the My Brother's Keeper initiative to bring together cities, towns, businesses, and foundations that are taking important steps to connect our young people to the types of mentoring, support, networks, and skills development they need to find good jobs. This initiative was launched to help Black and other youth of color devise individualized plans of action to prepare them for college and to work their way into the middle class. In addition to these efforts, however, Godly African American men must play a part in cultivating a spiritual life that will complement the skill sets such programs hope to establish. Our Black Elijahs and Elishas of today must reeducate themselves about the mantle that is theirs to carry and recognize the power that God gives to those who carry that mantle faithfully.

We Black men can choose either to embrace the mantle of manhood or reject it and be vulnerable to the consequences of our disobedience. If we choose to embrace our mantle, we accept the belief that within every man is a constant reminder of what God intended the Christian life to be. All our Elijahs need an Elisha, and every Elisha needs an Elijah. Truth be told, every Elisha struggles with a hidden weakness or fragility that he hopes an Elijah will provide him with the strength he needs to overcome. When a young Elisha becomes a man, blessed with strength and time-tested wisdom, he gains humility knowing it is not his strength but that which he was blessed with by the Elijahs in his life. Is there a more accurate portrait of what the Christian life should be like?

Though the temptation is huge for Black men of God to declare ourselves strong, independent, and self-made, real fulfillment comes only upon recognizing that it is Christ's strength, in us and through us, that makes us who and what we are. We need to reclaim the mantle of manhood in our communities to ensure that when our Elishas become old they do not reject the humble acknowledgment of their dependence upon Christ, who is the ultimate source of their strength. Black men of God, God's mantle is on *you*!

CONSEQUENCE

When men of God choose to embrace the mantle of manhood, four things generally tend to happen: *prayer*, *prophetic proclamation*, *participation*, and *praise*.

Prayer. The Hebrew word *tefilah* (תפילה) generally is translated in English as the word we commonly know as "prayer." Scholars suggest, however, that it is a mistake to assume that prayer simply means begging, beseeching, or imploring God for one's daily needs. Prayer is actually a commandment that God demands all His children to observe. It is through prayer that we turn to God for help and, in times of comfort, show our gratitude for who God is and for what He has done. It is the language we use to submit our humble petitions to God. It is through the realm of prayer that God makes known to the mantle-bearers His intended purpose for their lives. As affirmed in 1 Timothy 2:8: "Therefore I want the men everywhere to pray, lifting up holy hands without anger or disputing." God affirms the life of the mantle-bearer who prays.

Prophetic Proclamation. God does not call those whom He wants to pray to remain silent; rather, He intends for the prayerful to be powerful and prophetic in their public speech. Prophetic proclamation is a spiritual weapon that can be used to destroy the systems of the world that oppress the poor and the downtrodden. We Black men of God must use it against the rulers, powers, forces of darkness, and spiritual wickedness that work to undermine the sanctity and integrity of our communities. We who know we have a mantle to bear must have the power to speak, and we must speak into existence those things that are not as though they were. Whether we are teaching, preaching, or providing demonstrative acts of faith through the lifestyles we live, we must be mindful that our words—when we align our will with God's will—are both impactful and prophetic. As Titus 2:1 says: "You, however, must teach what is appropriate to sound doctrine."

Participation. Not only must a Black man of God be equipped to prophesize, but he must also be willing to participate in his own deliverance. Verses 19-20 in 1 Kings 19 reveal that Elisha was a hard worker before Elijah showed up in his life. He worked with oxen to farm his land, and apparently, he was good at it, based upon the number of oxen mentioned in the text. Even though the land had fallen under the idolatrous regime of Ahab and Jezebel, Elisha worked hard to turn a profit in an unprofitable situation. This is the type of character God admires in men who are willing to work. No social or political revolution can take place unless men demonstrate their willingness to put their hands to the plow. Too many of us Black men are standing idly by, waiting for an Elijah to come and put his mantle upon our shoulders before we show a willingness to work hard for the kingdom of God. "But the one who joins himself to the Lord is one spirit with Him." (1 Corinthians 6:17)

Praise. Psalm 150:6 makes it very clear that God's entire created order ought to praise its Creator! Men who have been chosen to carry a mantle are also chosen to give God praise. Praise not only conveys to God the notion that one is thankful for what God has done in times past, it also conveys to God the notion that one is thankful for what God intends to do in the future. As men who have been called and chosen to carry the mantle of mentorship, loving compassion, and spiritual direction, Black Christian men can praise God in advance, knowing that He would not choose us if He did not intend to equip us and change the world through us. As written in Psalm 35:28: "And my tongue shall speak of your righteousness and of your praise all day long."

As godly Black men with mantles to pass on, we must reclaim our commitment to prayer, prophetic proclamation, participation, and praise. We must teach our young men that the change we seek begins with us, like the mustard seed that grows out of our commitment to reshaping the context in which it has been planted. The mantle of God will equip an Elijah who sings with a Sam Cooke flow to connect to the soul of an Elisha who walks with a lean like Kendrick Lamar.

Let the record be set straight: men with a mantle reach up to their God, reach out to their neighbors, and reach down to help those of future generations to rise. Men with a mantle know how to transcend cultural differences and generational barriers to reclaim a hope for the future and an alternative reality for the downtrodden and the oppressed. Black men of God, God's mantle is on *you*!

CHALLENGE

Every man feels within him a sense that he is working at a deficit when trying to overcome the multitude of injustices in the world. This sense of inadequacy only intensifies when a man feels as though he is alone in his community, with no voice of strength to turn to for support. In the worst of times, such lonely men will masquerade in public as having inner tranquility and a sense of complete control over their destinies. In private, they often are fearful, deeply troubled, and wrestling with insecurities about their masculinity. Much like Elijah, even the best of God's chosen men grows weary from the journey and can become desperate, if not disenchanted, with their limited capacity to bring about meaningful change in their communities.

The challenge for today's Black man of God is that he must believe that he walks with a mantle of leadership. Much like Elisha, African American Christian men must convince themselves that they have been called to participate in God's redemptive plan to restore peace, righteousness, and justice to the land. We must trust that our unique qualities as men of faith are what separate us from every other type of man, and that our mantle is enough to restore order to the places the world has labeled as chaotic. Black men of God, God's mantle is on *you*!

The story of Elijah and Elisha in 1 Kings 19:19-21 reminds us that God is our ultimate security, strength, and refuge. No amount of bondage, overwhelming weakness, or personal struggle can challenge God's unending sufficiency and perfect love. Yes, fundamentally speaking, it is true that a man needs security, strength, refuge, and identity; his community needs this as well, as does his family. That is why God often chooses to place His mantle upon the shoulders of His chosen men—men like Elijah and Elisha—to affirm in the hearts of the next generation that their foundation and future in Christ will remain secure. Black men are needed to lead prayer walks in all our communities. They are needed to lead prayer at the dinner tables in all our homes. They are needed to attend PTA meetings in all our schools and to safeguard all the basketball, football, baseball and soccer games being played in all our public parks and recreation centers.

To be clear, God does not exclude our godly Black women from the sharing the burden of carrying the mantle of leadership in our communities. The legacy of great women leaders like Sojourner Truth, Ida B. Wells, Rosa Parks, Fannie Lou Hamer, Dorothy Height, and Coretta Scott King dispel such notions. Notwithstanding, African American communities are most potent and robust with prophetic movements when the Elijahs and Elishas of each generation are on call and actively engaged in the work of liberation for all God's people. Black men of God, God's mantle is on *you*!

CHRISTOLOGICAL PRINCIPLE

> *"So, Jesus said to them again, 'Peace be with you; as the Father has sent Me, I also send you.' And when He had said this, He breathed on them and said to them, 'Receive the Holy Spirit....'"* (John 20: 21-22)

When Jesus blew his breath upon his disciples in much the same way Elijah covered Elisha with his cloak, Jesus prophetically released his mantle unto the disciples, along with the power it wielded. The full manifestation of this mantle became evident on the day of Pentecost, when the Holy Spirit (the mantle) fell upon the disciples, and they began to walk with supernatural powers. Similarly, we followers of Christ have all been given the mantle of the Holy Spirit to walk in peace, forgiveness, and oneness with God.

CRISIS

Regrettably, we today live in a day and time when God's mantle is equated with material gain more so than spiritual restoration. We are bearing witness to the emergence of a pseudo-Christianity which suggests that God's mantle is something that can be put on or discarded on a whim. No longer is the mantle of God viewed as something that is intricately a part of us and that shapes the core of who we are. In today's world, the mantle of God is often viewed as a downloadable product filtered by our arrogance or controlled by our self-centeredness.

Many today say to God, "I'll obey you, but on my terms. I'll go there, but at my pace. I'll preach it, but in my own way. I'll do it, but when I think the time is right." One of the reasons the mantle of God has become so burdensome to so many of us is because we think that we have the right to tell God how we think God should be working through us, yet no radical movement or change can occur in our lives, communities, societies, or world unless we yield totally to the mantle of God. No spiritual renewal will come about without our total submission to the will of the Holy Spirit. There are times when we have to accept that our way can only take us so far. There comes a point in life when only a total yielding to the Holy Spirit will produce the type of change, we desire in our homes and communities. Black men of God, God's mantle is on *you*!

COVENANT

When Elisha slaughters the oxen that had previously provided his livelihood, he makes a powerful statement of vocational commitment. For Elisha, there is no going back to his former way of life. No longer will he live just for himself. Elisha recognizes that his submission to God will not only have an impact on him and his immediate family but also on his entire nation, out of which God chose him specifically.

The question we Black men of God must ask ourselves is, "What is God calling me to do today? What is God asking me to give up? What's at stake if I choose to reject the mantle God wants to place upon my life?" We must reclaim the roles of prayer intercessors, protectors, providers, mentors, teachers, preachers, and prophets. We must not only reclaim our places as the watchmen who sit on the walls of our communities but also assume the role of priests who walk with, not above, our communities in total communion with God.

CONCLUSION

1. Mantles are meant to be transferred between generations.

2. God is still calling Black men of faith to embrace the mantle of leadership that will enable them to partner with Him in the restoration of their communities.

3. Through Christ, we all have been given the mantle of the Holy Spirit to walk in peace, forgiveness, and oneness with God.

FIVE KEY SCRIPTURES

1. "He took the cloak that had fallen from Elijah and struck the water with it. 'Where now is the LORD, the God of Elijah?' he asked. When he struck the water, it divided to the right and to the left, and he crossed over." (2 Kings 2:14)

2. "And afterward, I will pour out my Spirit on all people. Your sons and daughters will prophesy, your old men will dream dreams, your young men will see visions." (Joel 2:28)

3. "But the Advocate, the Holy Spirit, whom the Father will send in my name, will teach you all things and will remind you of everything I have said to you." (John 14:26)

4. "For John baptized with water, but in a few days you will be baptized with the Holy Spirit." (Acts 1:5)

5. "When the day of Pentecost came, they were all together in one place. Suddenly a sound like the blowing of a violent wind came from heaven and filled the whole house where they were sitting. They saw what seemed to be tongues of fire that separated and came to rest on each of them." (Acts 2:1-3)

DIVE DEEPER

1. Discuss how difficult it is to pick up the mantle of manhood in a world that often rejects leadership coming from Black men.

2. How do you feel about current trends in society which suggest that manhood is defined by how much money you make?

3. Do you think it is possible to reignite dialogue between our young Black men and our older Black men? Do you think there is too much of a generational divide for mentorship to take place between the Elijahs and Elishas in our communities today?

4. Should Black men of God today be ashamed to accept the fact that they have a specific mantle to carry?

5. What are your feelings regarding the notion that every man needs an Elijah and an Elisha in his life?

6. Elijah was not intimidated by the fact that his work came with its own limitations. How do you feel about the fact that certain aspects of your work here on earth will remain unfinished? Explain.

APPLICATION

1. Regardless of how miniscule the task, everything God calls you to do is of immense importance to Him and His Kingdom. That is why we need the mantle, anointing, and commissioning of God to complete the tasks He has assigned to our lives.

2. There are certain tasks that only you can do. You were called to accomplish very specific tasks for God's glory. Whenever you feel as though such tasks are unachievable, remember that God not only called you but also prepared you to accomplish the assignment He gave you.

3. The mantle that we carry is not our own. Wisdom works best when it is shared between generations. Remember not only to remain faithful to what God calls you to accomplish, but also to pass on your experience, influence, and affluence to the generation that will come behind you.

AFFIRMATION

Lord, you chose me to carry the mantle of manhood during such as time as this. I will not abuse this mantle but will use it to empower a generation. I am mindful as well that this mantle is not my own. It belongs to God, and I cherish it as a God-given gift with a specific purpose and for a specific season.

SUPPLICATION

Lord, I am mindful that the anointing of Jesus is available to all of his followers and that his mantle is greater than any prophet in the Old Testament. It was Jesus who said, "Truly, truly, I say to you, he who believeth in me, the works that I do shall he do also; and greater works than these shall he do; because I go unto my Father" (John 14:12 KJV). Not only do I pray for the mantle of manhood to become activated in my life, I pray also for the mantle of Christ to make me more like You. May Your power manifest itself in my life like never before as I aim to walk with the authority of an Elisha and the passion to serve like an Elisha.

INVITATION

Jesus grants all who will follow him access to his mantle to accomplish works on this earth. Yet, seeking the "greater works" described in John 14:12 produces a specific outcome based upon the way each individual has been gifted. May you seek the mantle that God gifted for you specifically.

As you join in the struggle with your sisters and brothers, your giftedness will connect with and complement the giftedness of others in your community. Black men of God, God's mantle is on *you*!

MY BIBLE AND MY MENTOR:

Who's Your Mentor?

Dana Thompson,

Former Chair of the Deacon Board and Board of Directors, Oak Valley Baptist Church, Oak Ridge TN; President, Thompson Marketing Group; and Founding Member, Kingdom Men Inspires

Definition:

Mentor: A person who is looked to for wise advice and guidance; a wise and trusted counselor or teacher; an influential senior sponsor or supporter; an adviser, master, guide, preceptor.

Quote:

"Human beings, who are almost unique in having the ability to learn from the experience of others, are also remarkable for their apparent disinclination to do so."
— Douglas Adams (1952 – 2001),
staunch atheist and author of The Hitchhiker's Guide to the Galaxy

Scripture:

"The wise are mightier than the strong, and those with knowledge grow stronger and stronger. So, don't go to war without wise guidance; victory depends on having many advisers." (Proverbs 24:5-6)

"But you must remain faithful to the things you have been taught. You know they are true, for you know you can trust those who taught you. You have been taught the holy Scriptures from childhood, and they have given you the wisdom to receive the salvation that comes by trusting in Christ Jesus. All Scripture is inspired by God and is useful to teach us what is true and to make us realize what is wrong in our lives. It corrects us when we are wrong and teaches us to do what is right. God uses it to prepare and equip his people to do every good work." (2 Timothy 3:14–17)

CIRCUMSTANCE

Soon after I turned twenty-nine years old, I entered a new phase of my life, one for which I had no real experience. I felt overwhelmed, and I could not tell my wife how I felt because I had convinced her that our young family situation was perfect. What is a man to do when he realizes he is in over his head, and he has convinced others that he is not? Well, before I answer that question, let me fill you in on the details.

At the time, my wife and I had been married four-and-a-half years, and we had two young children. Our daughter was seven years old, and our son had just celebrated his first birthday. We had moved from Alabama to Massachusetts two years earlier. My family lived in California, and my wife's parents lived in Tennessee. Her brothers and sisters lived in Alabama and Georgia. We were just getting adjusted to life with two kids and no family being close enough to serve as a built-in support system. Then, suddenly, our small family grew—from two kids to twelve kids!

It all happened when we became resident directors for an ABC Community School Program in Topsfield, Massachusetts. ABC stands for A Better Chance (*www.abetterchance.org*), a program that provides talented but underprivileged, inner-city children of color with opportunities to attend excellent schools in suburban communities. Our ABC program was linked to Topsfield's Masconomet Regional High School, then ranked among the most competitive high schools in the country. Our ten new kids were boarding scholars in the program, which meant that during the school year, they lived full-time in a house subsidized by the local community, situated within the school's district, and supervised by two resident directors (my wife and I) and several tutors.

So, at the age of twenty-nine, I became a foster father of sorts for ten high school-aged young men from the inner cities of New York and New Jersey. After faking it for two months, I finally called my father, Charles T. Thompson, in California to ask him what I thought was a very difficult question: "How do you parent kids that aren't your own?" His answer was so simple, yet so profound. He said, "You can only parent one way. You have to parent them like they *are* your kids."

Then he told me the secret to effective parenting. "Good parenting," he said, "really consists of just three things. The first thing is setting a good example for your kids. The second thing is letting your kids know where you stand on the issues in life. And the third thing is praying. Oh, by the way, you should find yourself doing lots of the third thing!"

So, what's a man to do when he realizes he's in over his head and he's convinced others that he isn't? My solution: Call your mentor!

My father provided valuable insights and advice that year and during each of the following five years that my wife and I served as resident directors for the ABC Masconomet program. Sadly, four years after we left the program, my dad died. Brain cancer ended his life a month after his sixty-ninth birthday. At that time, I was thirty-nine years old and had started a computer consulting company that was beginning to take off. I was probably over my head again, but that time I did not have a mentor. Given the powerful impact my father's mentoring had in our success with the ABC program, what do you think I did? I looked for a new mentor!

I really did not want to ask for help again. In my mind, I was a mature, intelligent professional with lots of success in other endeavors, and I had a tough time admitting to myself that I needed guidance. Thus, the cycle of learning things the hard way began anew!

Can you relate?

CONFLICT

The way I see it, the problem for me and for other African American men is not necessarily a lack of mentors or potential mentors within our families, our church fellowships, our communities, or our workplaces. The problem is our unwillingness to submit ourselves to the process of being mentored. Being mentored, we so often believe, always costs us something, and instinctively we fear the cost is going to be high! Yet, the cost of being mentored is almost never a financial cost. More likely, it is the high cost of surrendering our will to Christ Jesus and one or more of His godly men. This is an extremely high price for most Black men to pay, even when we know the tremendous benefits of true mentorship.

After my father passed away, I found it increasingly difficult to humble myself and pay this price. I realize now that God did not intend for any man to be able to accomplish His purpose for our lives without the involvement of other saints. God has gifted each of us with many of the things we need to accomplish our purpose, yet it appears that all of God's leaders in the Bible have needed wise advice from others to accomplish their most important tasks. A couple of well-known examples come to my mind immediately.

Moses, for example, needed the wise counsel of his father-in-law Jethro on how to delegate and effectively manage his time and energy when leading God's people. The Apostle Paul needed the wise intervention of Barnabas to learn how to advance his ministry with the support of the disciples in Jerusalem. Therefore, two of God's most noteworthy leaders could not complete their mission without the help of their godly mentors.

It was a strange paradox for me. Though I was keenly aware of the tremendous benefits of having a mentor, I found it very uncomfortable to admit that I needed a mentor. Why was this, I asked myself? Can you relate?

CHOICE

What is a man to do BEFORE he gets in over his head? Proverbs 24:5-6 reminds us that Solomon found the answer: "The wise are mightier than the strong, and those with knowledge grow stronger and stronger. So, don't go to war without wise guidance; victory depends on having many advisers." Ephesians 6:12 explains that life itself is a war, a spiritual war against spiritual wickedness in high places. The enemy of mankind wants us to try to figure everything out on our own. Do not fall for that! Follow Solomon's advice! Get wise counsel from mentors who have succeeded in the endeavors you are about to begin!

About five years ago, I finally came to grips with the fact that I still needed mentors in my life. I was in the midst of putting together a new consulting company with four other men, and I became convicted about the need for mentoring. Not long afterward, that conviction led me to a business opportunity related to mentoring. Upon accepting my own need for mentors, I began to engage in serious study of the mentoring process as part of a profitable business opportunity for four years. It was so amazing to me to see how God will use something a person is interested in pursuing as bait for the thing He knows that person needs. God is smart! He knows how to move us in the direction of our blessings if we will only listen and obey.

Over time, I have learned that rejecting or ignoring the value of mentoring hinders progress in our homes, our careers, our churches, and our communities. Will you join me in making the choice to accept that you need mentors in your life? Will you also join me in the pursuit of understanding and profiting from the mentoring process?

CONSEQUENCE

A huge part of the problem regarding Black men and mentoring is that we do not—or will not—make time for the mentoring process within our busy lives. Making that time is a price we really do not want to pay. Why? Because we tend to have so little free time; we just want to hoard it for ourselves. We want to control that time. We do not even want Jesus to have our free time, and we definitely do not want to surrender it to another man!

About twenty-four years ago, I figured out who should be my primary mentor in this life: Jesus Christ. To gain the wisdom of my primary mentor, I had to make time for him. After long consideration of Paul's advice to Timothy in 2 Timothy 3:14-17, I eventually committed to reading a chapter of the Bible every morning. I have continued this practice ever since. It is an awesome way to start my day, with wise counsel, and I have accrued tremendous benefits over the years from that investment of my time each day!

I do the same for my other chosen mentors. I currently have three mentors besides Christ Jesus and the Holy Spirit. They are Rev. Dr. Larry Edmunds, Rev. Dr. Hardil Thomas, and Dr. William (Bill) Wright. They provide me with wise counsel in the areas of men's leadership development, organizational development, spiritual growth, and financial freedom. They have made themselves available to me for a number of years, but to gain the benefit of their experiences and wisdom, I have to commit to making time for them within my busy life.

Who are the mentors in your life that you need to make time for? Can you relate?

CHALLENGE

Not admitting one's need to be mentored and not making time to be mentored are big challenges, but they are not the biggest challenge. The biggest challenge is learning how to become effective mentors ourselves. If we submit ourselves to be mentored but do not then become mentors, the flow of wisdom stops with us. We may benefit, but the next generation is left wanting. We must get past our issues with mentoring and learn how to master the process of mentoring.

A mentor is anyone who has a beneficial, life-altering effect on another person, usually as a consequence of personal, one-on-one interactions. Mentors offer insight, perspective, knowledge, and wisdom that is useful to another person. The person who submits themselves to receiving the offered insight, perspective, knowledge, and wisdom of the mentor is called the protégé. Many of us have been mentoring others all our lives. We have also been protégés before. As mentors or protégés previously, we each participated in the progressive steps in the mentoring process, though we probably were not consciously aware of it. That process involves the following five steps: observing, intervening, partnering, performing, and reviewing.

Observing: Seeing the Behavior and Preparing for Intervention. The mentor sees something in the protégé which convinces him that the protégé could benefit from applying some of the things the mentor has learned through his life experiences. Sometimes, what the mentor sees is positive—for example, a strong work ethic or a positive, teachable attitude. Other times, what the mentor sees is negative—they may see a younger man heading down the wrong path or being influenced by people who do not have his best interests at heart. Often, a combination of both positive and negative attributes catches the mentor's attention. In any case, through observation, the mentor concludes that the protégé's behavior warrants an intervention on the mentor's part. Although the observation process usually takes considerable time, it is time well spent because a level of trust can be established. In some cases, the protégé will identify a potential mentor and initiate the start of the process. This start is still followed by a period of observation by the mentor, who is looking for evidence that he has something of value to contribute to the protégé before committing to the relationship.

Intervening: Making the Move to Establish the Relationship. The goal of intervention is for the protégé to accept the reality of his behavior. For the mentor to affect a change such as improved performance, the protégé has to want the mentor's advice. A foundation of trust must be established between the mentor and the protégé first. That foundation must be built on a solid relationship between the two men. To effectively intervene, the mentor must develop a strong bond with the protégé. Nevertheless, before great things can happen, both the mentor and the protégé must be willing to invest time in the relationship.

A man can only improve if he is self-motivated to change. He has to be willing to take risks and make the effort. The mentor-protégé relationship provides a safe environment for risk taking and is therefore a vital precursor for successful intervention.

Partnering: Developing a Partnership, Defining a Plan. The ability to move from the initial relationship to a partnership is the acid test of the mentoring process. When a partnership focused on helping the protégé achieve his specific goals has been formed, an environment for risk taking is established. The mentor is able to hold the protégé accountable for results and behavior based on trust rather than positional authority. At that point, the mentor and protégé can begin establishing an action plan for change. A mentoring relationship without specific goals does not produce lasting change, and goal setting is the basis for the final two steps in the mentoring process. The mentor and protégé should jointly devise a plan for achieving the desired goals including a tracking system for measuring progress and a reward-and-recognition system for celebrating victories. They likewise must both commit to executing that plan.

Performing: Executing the Plan, Mentoring for Performance. To effect change and improvement, thought must become action. The protégé begins acting on the advice of his mentor through the activities outlined in the action plan. His goal is to improve his performance in the areas specified. The mentor encourages the protégé's action and monitors his performance. Engaging in constant challenge, interaction, performance, and feedback is where the mentor-protégé relationship rubber meets the road, and it is made possible by the strong bonds of trust developed in the intervening and partnering steps.

Reviewing: Tracking Performance and Providing Feedback. The reviewing step is actually one of recognition and affirmation. As one of the oldest management axioms known to business states: "Things that get measured get done." We humans thrive on this type of structured feedback. Effective mentor-protégé relationships allow new behaviors and skills to be learned and maintained under schedules of reinforcement and rewards. It is the mentor's responsibility to constantly provide feedback to the protégé, to measure his performance on a regular basis and establish regular times for providing feedback.

The following guidelines are useful when providing feedback to a protégé:

- Be specific.

- Ask questions to help the protégé discover solutions.

- As much as possible, give feedback face-to-face.

- Check for understanding and ask for next steps (e.g., "What will you do differently next time?")

That's it! Five steps to affect changes that strengthen families, careers, businesses, churches, and communities. If the mentor-protégé relationship remains strong at the end of the cycle, the cycle repeats again and again. New behaviors are observed, interventions are recommended, and the protégé is off and running once more toward performance improvement.

We can develop new mentors in our families, our businesses, our churches, and our communities by employing the "each-one-teach-one" methodology. First, teach others to mentor, then teach those mentors to pass on the wisdom received from their mentors to other deserving protégés out there.

I am committed to doing my part. I have resolved to pass on the insight, perspective, knowledge, and wisdom of my mentors to others by writing three books, which I have tentatively titled:

- *An African American Father's Secrets for Successful Parenting*

- *African American Leadership: Embracing the Mentor Role*

- *Mentorship Submission: The Path to Black Male Empowerment*

What are you prepared to do? Now that you've been exposed to these five steps, commit to taking a little time to study them. Then, teach them to other men.

CHRISTOLOGICAL PRINCIPLE

Mark 10:42-44, NLT quotes Jesus as saying, "You know that the rulers in this world lord it over their people, and officials flaunt their authority over those under them. But among you it will be different. Whoever wants to be a leader among you must be your servant, and whoever wants to be first among you must be the slave of everyone else."

Jesus intended men to mentor one another, not lord over one another. Every Godly man within God's church fellowship has some life experiences that could be useful to at least one other man within that fellowship. A man can open himself up to mentorship when he humbles himself and believes his mentor will act according to Christ's servant-leader model, as described in the text above. As potential mentors and protégés of Godly mentors, we must humble ourselves for the mentoring process to be effective.

CRISIS

Our families, our churches, and our communities need more men to step up and become mentors. Many African American men find themselves in situations where they are in over their heads. They need a mentor to help guide them through their challenges.

Have you learned anything in this life that could be of value to someone else? Can you be a mentor? Will you step up and stand in the gap for your brothers and for the next generation?

COVENANT

I will humble myself and seek wise counsel in the areas of marriage, fatherhood, business or career, church leadership, and community leadership. Will you do the same?

CONCLUSION

1. ASK JESUS TO BE YOUR PRIMARY MENTOR and then ask Him to lead you to other mentors.

2. BECOME AWARE of the importance and impact of a mentor in your life and in the life of someone else.

3. REALIZE you have a responsibility to share your experiences with others as a mentor.

4. DECIDE to become a mentor to a younger man in your church or neighborhood.

FIVE KEY SCRIPTURES

1. "And I myself also am persuaded of you, my brethren, that ye also are full of goodness, filled with all knowledge, able also to admonish one another." (Romans 15:14 KJV)

2. "For, brethren, ye have been called unto liberty; only use not liberty for an occasion to the flesh, but by love serve one another." (Galatians 5:13 KJV)

3. "Let the word of Christ dwell in you richly in all wisdom; teaching and admonishing one another in psalms and hymns and spiritual songs, singing with grace in your hearts to the Lord." (Colossians 3:16 KJV)

4. "Not forsaking the assembling of ourselves together, as the manner of some is; but exhorting one another: and so much the more, as ye see the day approaching." (Hebrews 10:25 KJV)

5. "Likewise, ye younger, submit yourselves unto the elder. Yea, all of you be subject one to another, and be clothed with humility: for God resisteth the proud, and giveth grace to the humble." (1 Peter 5:5 KJV)

DIVE DEEPER

1. Identify three men who could become valuable mentors in your life if they knew your need.

2. What can we do to make time in our busy lives so that our mentors can engage with us?

3. Discuss a time when you observed a younger man whom you realized could benefit from your life experiences. What did you observe that convinced you that they could benefit from your insight, perspective, knowledge, and wisdom?

4. What is it that God wants you to do that will require a mentor's insights to help you do it? Explain.

5. What situations in your community could be improved through mentoring relationships? Explain.

6. I cannot be mentored if I won't humble myself. Do I act like a know-it-all at times?

7. I cannot be mentored if I am too heavy to be lifted up. Do others find it hard to work with me?

8. Mentors can be trusted to help instead of hinder. Do others consider me a good team member, someone who can be trusted to serve the team? Explain.

9. Mentors have to understand the situation before they can give wise counsel. Do others consider me a good listener? Explain.

APPLICATION

1. Set a good example. Learn the five steps in the mentoring process and teach them to a least one other person within the next two months.

2. Let others know where you stand on important life issues. Commit to mentoring a younger person for the next twelve months. Meet with them for at least one hour a week.

3. Pray! Pray that God will raise up new mentors within your community to invest their wisdom in this next generation. Call another man at least once each month for the next year and pray together for mentors in your church and your community.

AFFIRMATION

Lord, you have given me access to your wisdom through your Word, through the guidance of the Holy Spirit, and through godly mentors within the fellowship. Today, I am going to humble myself and seek your wisdom from all three sources.

SUPPLICATION

Lord, by Your wisdom You founded this earth. I am destined to encounter situations on this earth for which I am unprepared, and I need Your wisdom to guide me. I pray for Your wisdom to help me to be Your servant-leader in my home, my local church, and my community. Protect me and the other men in my local church fellowship from the tendency to lean unto our own understanding. Help us to trust in You and to acknowledge You in all our ways. Then, You shall be able to direct our paths as you have promised. This I pray, in Jesus' name. Amen.

INVITATION

I invite you to join me in letting Christ be your mentor. Let Him mentor you through His Word, through the Holy Spirit's guidance, and through the wisdom of the brothers in Christ that He has provided within the fellowship to mentor us from their life experiences!

MY BIBLE AND MY MARRIAGE:

Cleave to Achieve

Stanley E. Harris,

Deacon, Mt. Olivet Baptist Church, Columbus OH

Definition:

Marriage: the covenant and purpose of the union of man and woman

Quote:

> *"Love is one long, sweet dream and marriage is the alarm clock."*
> — Anonymous

Scripture:

"And the Lord God said, It is not good that the man should be alone; I will make him an help meet for him. And the Lord God caused a deep sleep to fall upon Adam, and he slept: and he took one of his ribs and closed up the flesh instead thereof; And the rib, which the Lord God had taken from man, made he a woman, and brought her unto the man. And Adam said, This is now bone of my bones, and flesh of my flesh: she shall be called Woman, because she was taken out of Man. Therefore, shall a man leave his father and his mother, and shall cleave unto his wife: and they shall be one flesh. And they were both naked, the man and his wife, and were not ashamed." (Genesis 2:18; 21–25)

CIRCUMSTANCE: THE ESSENCE OF THE CENTRAL PROBLEM

The book of Genesis states that, after God finished His work of creation, He created man, named him Adam, and charged him to have dominion over all He had created. He placed Adam in a special place, the Garden of Eden and gave him the mandate to dress and keep the garden. As Genesis 1:31 concludes, "God saw everything that He had made, and, behold, it was very good," and God rested the next day.

After giving Adam his various responsibilities, Genesis continues, God noticed that Adam was "alone." He saw that Adam was singular in his approach to God's work and to the responsibilities assigned to him. He also saw that Adam had no one to share the garden with, no one to procreate with so he could multiply, and no one to assist with replenishing and subduing all the other creatures on the earth. God then decided that this was "not good."

When one considers that God previously had concluded that everything, He had made was very good, and that He had assessed Adam's aloneness as not good, a critical issue arises—one that begs further analysis. Why, for instance, did God have a problem with Adam being alone? One can only surmise that God, in His infinite wisdom, knew that Man could not multiply or reproduce by himself. Moreover, God knew that even in the most ideal situation, Adam's ability to dominate, replenish, and subdue the earth's creatures, even to dress the garden, were tasks to be shared. God also decided, however, that nothing else He had created up to that point would suffice in solving Adam's aloneness. We know this because later, in Genesis 2:19-20, God presented the creatures He made to Adam, "but for Adam there was not found a help meet for him." Notice that this was not an issue for Adam, it was an issue identified, defined, and ultimately resolved by God. Adam merely, as the popular phrase states, 'goes along to get along.'

Genesis makes clear God understood that for man to begin to multiply, a way to reproduce over and over had to be established. Once that was in place, God reasoned, man (collectively) would need to govern himself and create culture and mores by which to live civilly and in community with each other. Thus, God's creative purpose, from the beginning, involved both male and female. Genesis goes on to say that God tasked His male and female humans with the responsibility of being fruitful. They were also commanded to multiply as well as to replenish and subdue all the creatures on the earth.

CONFLICT

Unlike His creations in the animal kingdom, God intended man and woman, as partners, to exhibit more than just sexual instinct. The conflict that the marriage partnership helps to resolve is one God addressed in His conclusions about man and his aloneness—namely, the conflict associated with Adam "going solo." I like to call this the Me, Myself and I Syndrome, which encompasses Adam's response to discovering and accepting the woman God created to eliminate man's aloneness. Adam understood the woman's personhood and saw her as his equal. He further understood her purpose and role as his partner and helper and accepted her as a gift from God. This partnership implies a unity in which each helps the other equally. It is an essential part of what the Bible describes as cleaving to become one flesh.

This apparent conflict continues to reverberate in societies' cultures, mores, and laws. Gender discrimination, even that regarding the most basic of rights, has been a societal issue in nearly every culture, country, and government in history. It is an ongoing issue in American society and government today, where men are struggling to accept women as their equals, and in many cases, continue to belittle, berate, and dumb-down the helper/help meet role for which woman was created. In recent years, this conflict has played out with women retaliating against men's group and individual humiliation by rejecting the helper/help meet role, deciding to remain single, or yoking to another woman in a lesbian relationship.

The escalating rates of out-of-wedlock pregnancy are yet another sign of the breakdown in understanding between men and women in America and ultimately men's dumbing down and women's rejection of the helper/help meet role. Too many young men and woman in our society today mistake pregnancy as a consequence of sexual intercourse as opposed to it being part of the purpose of sexual intimacy. In the former situation, generally speaking, neither the man nor the woman planned to procreate. Procreation is seen instead as an unintended consequence. This generally leads to unnecessary and unholy conflict among the couple, their families, and the children who are born into and who struggle to get through the chaos resulting from such circumstances.

It is small wonder that our urban communities have disintegrated largely into isolated societies of violence, illiteracy, poverty, and immorality at all levels. A resolution to this divisive conflict would be to lay the groundwork for men to develop a system, process, and structure to reproduce (but not clone) ourselves, to govern ourselves civilly, and to create culture and mores pleasing to God.

CHOICE

When God determined that it was not good for Adam to live alone, while attempting to do God's will unassisted, Adam was "all in." He did not dispute, fight, argue, or even question God as to whether he personally was bothered by his aloneness. There was no hint that Adam was uncomfortable being alone. There was no evidence of his loneliness or even feelings of lack of friendship. What the Bible says is that God said it was not good for Adam to be alone.

My supposition is that God's insight and foresight into the life possibilities He intended for Adam revealed that it was not in Adam's best interest to go it alone in his quest to dominate, replenish, and subdue the earth, battle Satan, and reproduce. Those responsibilities God chose to assign to both male and female. Likewise, God surmised, it was not in Adam's best interest to be placed in the Garden of Eden, in all its splendor and plenty, and not have the privilege and joy of sharing it with someone, both in its maintenance and in the enjoyment of the fruit produced. Nor was it in Adam's best interests, God determined, for him to go it alone in the formation of communities, cultures, and mores.

Man needed help—help that God knew only a God-selected helper/help meet could provide. He created woman expressly for that role, and Adam accepted God's pronouncement of same. When Eve was presented to him, Adam trusted God. He had faith that God had provided him with the helper/help mate that God knew he needed. Adam did not ask for a variety of women to choose from or even a single additional choice from which to choose. Adam did not accept the woman because she was beautiful (although I am sure she was). He did not accept her because she was well-connected, well-bred, well-fed, or well-read. Rather, he accepted her as a gift from God and understood that God created her by removing a part of his body.

Adam saw her as his equal. He saw the connection. He saw her as a complement to him. Ultimately, Adam saw the partnership/relationship/covenant God intended between God, Adam, and the uniquely created being He calls woman. Adam did not choose Eve, but he accepted her for whom God made her to be—a help mate and partner in doing the work of God. Adam accepted God's intent. This is evident in Adam's response to God after Eve was presented to him: "This (woman) is now bone of my bone," Adam concludes, "and flesh of my flesh." Implied in all of this is the biblical notion that "not my will but Thy will be done."

Proverbs 3:5-6 is confirmation that Adam understood the need to "Trust in the Lord with all thine heart; and lean not unto thine own understanding. In all thy ways acknowledge Him, and he shall direct thy paths." God, however, presented Eve to Adam to see if she was acceptable to him as his helper/help meet. He gave Adam a choice, and that choice did not just include whether or not to accept the gift of the woman but also to choose or reject her role as his helper/help meet and the partnership/relationship/covenant it entailed. Adam chose Eve, her role, and the covenant. He cleaved to her.

CONSEQUENCE

As soon as Adam accepted Eve, God instituted marriage through the following scriptural pronouncement: "Therefore shall a man leave his father and his mother and shall cleave unto his wife; and they shall be one flesh." (Genesis 2:24) And with the advent of marriage, Adam's life—and our world—changed forever.

Though God did not Himself make the above statement, scripture, in its declaration, makes it clear that it is God's intent. A big part of this declaration is the notion that a man should marry or covenant to be with the woman God presents to him and subsequently leave his father and mother after he accepts that woman—trusting that God has made her to be the unique helper/help meet he needs to do God's work and fulfill God's will for his life.

In American society generally, even within the African American community, and in the African American church specifically, fulfilling God's will too often slips to the bottom of men's priority list, if it makes that list at all. This impacts how we men select our helpers/help meets and how we view the helper/help meet role generally. Yet, because we do not allow God to lead and drive that process, we typically utilize the wrong process, select a mate for the wrong reasons, and then enter into covenant with her without including God as a party to that covenant. We just ask him to *bless the union.*

CHALLENGE

The challenges thus are threefold. First, we as men must meet the challenge of understanding both the role and the assignment God has for our lives. We need to pursue a deeper knowledge of God and His Son Jesus Christ, Savior of the world. As in the beginning, we need to understand that God has the whole world in His hands. He made the world and everything therein, He oversees and orchestrates the events and circumstances of our lives, and He has our individual and collective best interests at heart. God has pinpointed an assignment for every man, and He has custom-fitted us to fulfill His plan for our lives. Moreover, He makes available to us all the provisions necessary for success in fulfilling our God-given roles. He will provide a helper for us, if and when, He deems it wise. We do not need to hunt down, shop for, experiment, or test potential candidates! We do not need our friends or relatives to try to arrange for us to meet our potential mate or provide matchmaking services.

Second, God has issued the challenge that man, and woman should cleave one to the other and become "one flesh." This cleaving is marriage between husband and wife: one man to one woman. It is not man to man nor woman to woman (homosexuality); neither is it about marrying as many mates as one wants (polygamy). The creation story (Genesis 2:24) tells of God's plan that husband and wife should be one. Further, in Ephesians 5:28-29a NIV, Paul says: "In this same way, husbands ought to love their wives as their own bodies. He who loves his wife loves himself. After all, no one ever hated his own body." Paul further states that every man must love his wife as he loves himself, specifically suggesting that:

1. a husband should be willing to sacrifice everything for his wife;

2. a husband should make his wife's well-being a matter of primary importance;

3. the union of husband and wife merges two persons in such a way that little can affect one without also affecting the other, and that each one helps the other become all he or she can be.

Third, God challenges both men and women to understand that cleaving to each other is ultimately the key to personal and collective success. God intends for men and women, as husbands and wives, to cleave together to achieve their greatest good. Through such unions, we can impact our homes, our communities, our societies, our nations, and the world positively. When a man and a woman come together physically, mentally, and emotionally as one body in covenant with God, they give their children, born out of their intimacy with each other, the best chance for success and achievement. The intimacy between a husband and wife is physical, emotional, and spiritual.

When the two, as one, are in covenant with God, their relationship with each other, with Him, and with their family means something special. There is no room for rape, physical, mental or psychological abuse, or sexual discrimination. The union, the covenant, and the relationship are worth sacrificing for, working hard for, providing for, and doing whatever it takes to preserve and protect. The desire for this covenant union is what drives the Christian man's ambition, volition, morality, and ethic. Through such a union, we men have the best chance to achieve the familial, societal, and cultural relationships God envisions for us.

CHRISTOLOGICAL PRINCIPLE

As Christ responded to the Pharisees when they asked Him about divorce, "Haven't you read that at the beginning the Creator 'made them male and female,' and said 'For this reason a man will leave his father and mother and be united to his wife, and the two will become one flesh?'" Jesus knew that God meant for man and woman to join so that they would no longer be two, but of one flesh. "Therefore," He said, "what God has joined together, let no one separate." (Matthew 19:4-6)

This cleaving or joining one to another is meant to be everlasting, just as our relationship with God the Father, Jesus the Son and our Lord, and the Holy Spirit is meant to be. There is a power in these unions that is far greater than the power of the individual and sufficient in strength to carry us all in battle against Satan and all the evil forces that seek to conquer, divide, and destroy us.

CRISIS

Relationships between men and women are in trouble today for many reasons. Chief among these is that there simply is not enough teaching, preaching, and modeling in spiritually healthy male-female relationships. Our communities, especially our church communities, do not do enough to teach the principles of spiritual matrimony. Spiritual matrimony is a marital covenant that promotes seeking the will of God for our lives, doing the will of God as part of our ambition, and letting God direct our efforts in choosing a mate, a vocation, and a godly lifestyle.

The Old Testament writers and prophets continuously warned the Israelites about being unevenly yoked—that is, marrying persons who worshipped a different god and who had different beliefs, and who engaged in different religious practices, rituals, and customs. We hardly discuss this concept within Christian circles today. Too many of our young girls are attracted to the "bad boy" or "gangsta" characters. Too many of our young men grow up thinking that intelligence, good grades, and Christian character are "geekish" and "old school" and therefore out of date and unacceptable. Too many of our young adults and teenagers hardly know anyone who is legally married anymore, not to mention men and women who are spiritually yoked, cleaved, and in covenant with God.

Often, today's young people are conflicted when their preachers or Sunday school teachers talk about homosexuality as a sin. They are supportive of civil unions and same-sex marriage and view those arrangements as wholly acceptable to God simply because they have not been taught any better. Shacking up and living in common-law arrangements are so common and Hollywood-acceptable, that our young people today question even the need for marriage, much less the need for a man and a woman to commit to one another. This crisis is wreaking havoc in our homes, communities, churches, cultures, and societies. It is destroying our very sense of morality.

COVENANT

The word *covenant*, according to the 1996 edition of *Vines Expository Dictionary of Old and New Testament Words*, signifies "a mutual undertaking between two parties or more, each binding himself to fulfill obligations. It does not in itself contain the idea of joint obligation, it mostly signifies an obligation undertaken by a single person" (p. 242-243). The covenant between Adam and Eve and God was mutual, binding each to fulfill obligations. Adam and Eve committed each to be a helper to the other and to do the will of God as an obligation to Him. This meant more than sticking and staying "through thick and thin, sickness and health"—words generally uttered as part of traditional marriage vows. It meant each shared a commitment to work together to help the other fulfill his or her respective roles and purposes in carrying out the will of God. It signified a binding obligation to trust God in the decision to come together in covenant with Him in marriage, to trust that God accepts the two as helpers for each other, and to trust that God not only blesses the union but actually ordains it. It involved a public declaration by each to trust God to lead and guide the relationship to do the will of God. It entailed an obligation on the part of one man and one woman to live together for God, *forever*.

CONCLUSION

God ordained marriage, defined as the coming together of man and woman in covenant with God, principally to solve Adam's "aloneness" issue. The helper/help meet role entrusted to women is meant to be a blessing for both husband and wife and their relationship with God. It is the foundation upon which all other human relationships are based. Therefore, to misunderstand or underestimate the importance of marriage, of man and woman cleaving—one to another to become one flesh—is, according to Baltimore's esteemed Rev. P. M. Smith, to "miss the boat on God's idea of relationship." As Rev. Smith further contends: "If it ain't about [that] relationship, it ain't about nothing!"

FIVE KEY SCRIPTURES

1. "Every wise woman buildeth her house: but the foolish plucketh down with her hands." (Proverbs 14:1)

2. "A man's heart deviseth his way: but the Lord directeth his steps." (Proverbs 16:9)

3. "House and riches are the inheritance of fathers: and a prudent wife is from is from the Lord. Proverbs." (19:14)

4. "Favor is deceitful, and beauty is vain: but a woman that feareth the Lord, she shall be praised." (Proverbs 31:30)

5. Two are better than one: because they have a good reward for their labor. Ecclesiastes (4: 9)

DIVE DEEPER

1. Discuss which dating elements can lead to marriage.

2. Discuss the impact of combining personal finances in marriage.

3. Do you believe God will lead you to a helpmate of whom your family will not approve?

4. What do you think you must do to position yourself so that God will reveal your helpmate to you?

5. Do you believe God will ordain a marriage and each of its partners after they have married devoid of forging an initial covenant with God?

6. How does marriage between a man and woman in covenant with God affect the community in which they live?

7. Can you explain to your wife or significant other how the two of you can be helpmates to each other?

8. What is your commitment to God on behalf of your helpmate?

APPLICATION

God showed woman (Eve) to Adam (man). You should trust God enough to believe that He will show you the woman He created for you as your helper/help meet. God is an awesome God! Be careful with whom you covenant in partnership with Him! Thank God because He will create a helper *and* a special person you can help—*one and the same*—just for you!

AFFIRMATION

Lord, I am grateful for *all* you have done for me. I am especially grateful for my helper/help meet. I will cherish and honor her for who she is!

SUPPLICATION

Lord, I honor You in Your sovereignty, and I adore You in Your infinite wisdom and love. I thank You for my marriage to and relationship with my wife and helper/help meet. I praise Your blessed name for allowing my help meet and me to cleave one to another, strive to become one flesh, and strive to live to the Glory of God Almighty. Please continue to strengthen and protect our sacred covenant with You and with each other forever. Amen

INVITATION

God is all about relationships. He wants to be in right relationship with each of us. That right relationship is one in which we each must claim Him as both the Lord of our Lives and Savior from the many sins we have committed against Him. God promised never to leave us and to never leave us alone. I encourage you to stake your claim in Him, in right relationship, today and forever. Do so now, and you will never be alone. God Bless.

MY BIBLE AND MY METAMORPHOSIS:
He Changed Me

Dr. George W. Farmer Jr.,
Pastor, Olive Branch Baptist Church, Haymarket, VA

Definition:

Metamorphosis: A change of physical form; change of appearance or character; a supernatural transformation

Quote:

"If you would change to what you are not yet; you must be displeased with what you are. For where you were pleased with yourself, there you have remained. Keep adding, keep walking, keep advancing."
— Saint Augustine

Scripture:

"Therefore, if any man be in Christ, he is a new creature: old things are passed away; behold, all things are become new" (2 Corinthians 5:17 KJV).

CIRCUMSTANCE

Change does strange things to people. Perhaps, it is because we seldom want to deal with change in any fashion. Often, we do not want to face anything that requires us to adjust patterns of behavior that have become comfortable for us, nor do we want to face the uncertainties change naturally generates. Nonetheless, change is a constant force in all our lives. Without change, the world as we know it would cease to exist.

Change is often seen as a traumatic event to be avoided at all costs. Given a choice, most people would worship the status quo; however, to advance, improve, or accomplish anything, we must come face-to-face with change. Consequently, we must be willing to address the uncertainties, fears, and opportunities that change introduces into our lives. Otherwise, we will be left behind while the world moves ahead.

Churches in today's world also struggle with how to cope with and effect meaningful change. Unfortunately, far too many churches view change in the manner described in 2 Corinthians 12:7a—as a "thorn in the flesh" and "the messenger of Satan." In reality, change is the key to keeping churches vibrant and viable. Changes that are an integral part of a church's existence and that empower its congregation to maximize their potential must be leveraged to do the work of evangelism within their immediate environments. In addition, as part of their evangelism efforts—churches must be willing to make financial commitment to causes of other organizations that are beyond their immediate and respected vicinities.

Regrettably, too many pastors, as the titular leaders of their churches, fail to embrace and take charge of change. Consequently, they find themselves trying to put the proverbial "new wine" into old wineskins, only to experience an explosion because those old wineskins (the ways of the past) cannot accommodate the new wine (the substance of continuous change). As a result, change overwhelms and runs amok in the church, chaos, and uncertainty become the norm, and any hope of using change to take the church to new levels of success is discouraged. This is not a good situation. As pastors, we must learn to take charge of change to enhance our ability to lead our churches to the next level.

CONFLICT

As pastors, we must address a critical false element of change—namely, that it creates crisis and conflict. So many of us resistant change, yet all of us must change. The old rules become null and void when new paradigms or standards of operation shift. Those who cling to the past and to the status quo—I call them the Keepers of the Old Ways—will be left behind to choke on the dust of those who embrace change and move on. They will fight to hold on to what they know and what makes them comfortable. As a result, they will increasingly find themselves in untenable positions and subject to humiliating and confusing circumstances. To address the crises and conflict that change generates, today's pastors must be willing to embrace a New Order.

CHOICE

It is easy to talk about the need for change. It is more challenging to help others navigate the change process. Yes, there is a process for this, and learning how to apply that process to minimize the trauma change can cause is an important lesson.

Change almost always involves three stages: 1) Endings—the points at which we learn that the old ways cannot continue; 2) Neutral Zones—transitional stages experienced as one passes from the known into the unknown and is uncertain of the outcome; and 3) Beginnings—the periods during which one starts operating under new conditions, gaining confidence with each new experience.

Endings. Endings, or the points at which one gives up old ways of doing or being, always involve a grieving process much like experiencing the death of a loved one. In such cases, we may not want to give up what we had or what we found so comfortable, no matter what the future promises. We also may attempt to delay endings as long as we can, relinquishing our old ways—no matter how bad they were—with great reluctance. Sooner than later, however, endings are forced upon us if we refuse to accept them willingly. Consider the "Children of Israel" when they left Egypt, ending over four hundred years of slavery, and how they soon found themselves bemoaning their fates and longing for the security of their old lives.

Neutral Zones. Neutral zones are those intermediate periods through which we must pass when dealing with change. In many ways, these periods represent the toughest phases of the change process because no matter how much faith we have, we usually cannot see where we are going to end up when the change adventure is completed. This is a daunting prospect for most of us and a true test of our faith in many instances. The neutral zone experience can be likened to wandering around in a dark hallway in a strange building looking for a room that one is not certain is even in that building.

Those of us who serve as pastors must partner perseverance and courage with faith as we navigate this zone and guide our congregations along the path to change. This is a challenge that we, as leaders, must face, even as our decisions are challenged. Our followers may make unreasonable demands, and our options may appear confusing and deceptive, but we must be aware that ambiguity is a major, and regular, component of the neutral zone. Therefore, common sense often remains the best remedy. Of course, nothing is more uncommon than common sense.

Faith is what the Children of Israel were missing as they trekked through the desert. Though they knew what they had left behind, they had no concept of what was in store for them in the Promised Land. Consequently, they balked at the prospect of going to a new and unknown land. God punished them for their lack of faith by turning them back to the wilderness, where they wandered for thirty-nine years—all because they were unwilling to accept the change God offered them.

Beginnings. The reward for all who negotiate the neutral zones of change successfully is that they get to move on to new beginnings. New beginnings herald new ways to do things and new things to do. They are a sign that we have been able to cast off the old ways and embrace new and exciting approaches. They are testaments to the faith we must exercise as we negotiate the turmoil of change. Yet, upon arriving at our new beginnings, we learn that change is the only thing that never changes and that the change process is never-ending.

What happened to the Children of Israel is a prime example of the final stage of the change process. An entire generation had to die before the Israelites were ready to embrace the changes God had offered them years earlier. As they took on the challenge of beginning anew in the unknown territories of the Promised Land, they repeated the change cycle repeatedly, thus providing proof of the truth of the aphorism, *plus ça change, plus la même chose*: the more things change, the more they remain the same.

CONSEQUENCE

The change process, if we master it, enables us to address and deal with the new things that change brings. It takes courage and faith to deal with change, but the return for exercising that courage and walking by faith is the quantum change that takes place in us. In life, no one is offered any sense of certainty that his or her efforts will be well-received. We must learn that uncertainty is an integral part of the change process; it is always there and never leaves. How we manage the uncertainties of change determines whether we will overcome our fear of it and forge ahead to new heights of achievement.

CHALLENGE

Change follows and leads us, wherever we go. It is always, as the common expression maintains, "in the air." Indeed, change is evident in every aspect of our lives. As Heraclitus of Ephesus said: "All things change; nothing abides. Into the same river one cannot step twice." If change is so pervasive, then what is a person to do?

We face a real dilemma: change seldom seems to teach us anything. We generally seem to be so blissfully unaware that the world is changing around us. We ignore the "signs of the times" which tell us that the future will be different. And, no matter what happens, we typically react in the same way—by ignoring change until it overwhelms us. Then we look up and see that we have made the same mistakes our ancestors made.

The Qoheleth warned us in Ecclesiastes 1:9 that "there is nothing new under the sun." This statement presents us with a paradox, an oxymoron, and a puzzlement. If everything changes, how can there be nothing new under the sun? The answer is clear: We never seem to learn from the mistakes of the past; thus, we are doomed to repeat them. The major problem with this is that the consequences of our unaddressed errors increase with each new generation. We need to break this cycle of doom. To accomplish this, we must use the change we see happening around us to generate action. The actions and initiatives we undertake in the present must be strategically targeted to achieve positive changes in the future. We have no choice but to act.

But what should pastors, as leaders in the church, do? First, we must recognize that it is up to us to initiate change. Next, we must demonstrate the coping mechanisms our people need to adopt so they too can deal with change. This means that we must manage ourselves first. Action speaks louder than words. When the leader shows commitment to forging ahead through change, the people will follow. Does the fire inside you burn hot enough to ignite a flame in the hearts of your followers?

The ever-increasing pace of change has sent too many of us, leaders and followers alike, down a perilous path. In our fruitless quest for the urgent, the quick fix, we overlook the truly important elements of life. If we continue to make this mistake, the future will not offer much that any of us will want to see.

CHRISTOLOGICAL PRINCIPLE

Jesus is at the center of everything that is important in our respective lives. If we are to follow Christ, we must change from our old status to a new one. That is the primary reason change is so necessary. If we want to relate to Jesus, we must remember that Jesus told us—in so many ways—that He was the ultimate change agent. He fulfilled the entire law of God and refocused the theological emphases from strict obedience to unconditional love. We must change our spiritual focus and daily behaviors so that our lives too look like the life that Jesus lived while He walked this earth.

CRISIS

We cannot stop the world from changing. The best we can do is adapt to that change. Of course, smart people change before it is too late. Lucky people manage somehow to adjust to change, but only when "push comes to shove." The rest end up as losers and become history—but not in a good way. Part of the reason for this stratification is the entitlement mindset that has crept into public thinking over the past several decades. We cannot afford to fall into the trap of believing that we are entitled to anything—from pay raises to continued employment—even if we perform well. Instead, we need to "get right" with Jesus and reframe our relationship with the ever-changing world in which we live. We must put our faith in Christ, in the future, and in ourselves.

COVENANT

Jesus made a special covenant with his disciples when He told them, "In my Father's house are many mansions: if it were not so, I would have told you. I go to prepare a place for you. And if I go and prepare a place for you, I will come again, and receive you unto myself; that where I am, there ye may be also." (John 14:2-3) This covenant, which applies to all those of us who follow Christ, assumes that we have allowed the love of Jesus to change us. That is why Paul could write in 2 Corinthians 5:17: "Therefore if any man be in Christ, he is a new creature: old things are passed away; behold, all things are become new."

The Apostle John also captured the heart and soul of this covenant with Jesus when he wrote: "Beloved, now are we the sons of God, and it doth not yet appear what we shall be: but we know that, when He shall appear, we shall be like Him; for we shall see Him as he is." (1 John 2:2) In his pronouncement, John is telling us that, while we are here on earth, we are works in progress, constantly changing and being changed through the loving influence of the Holy Spirit. One day, when Jesus returns, this process of change will be complete, and we shall truly be "like Him"—mature and completely changed into a holy and sinless being.

CONCLUSION

When we trust and believe that Jesus will change us, we can be comfortable with and confident that He will orchestrate the changes necessary for us to be "like Him." We must, however, accept the challenges that come with this change process, which our theologians call sanctification, and commit to a continuing and progressive shift toward holiness. We must be willing to walk away from our old lives that are tinged with sin and destructive behaviors. We must shift our focus toward living lives that glorify our Lord and reconcile us to His very essence. Then we will be able to become God's "ambassadors" because we will be Christ's "representatives." Then God will use us to persuade other men and women to drop their differences and begin doing God's work.

FIVE KEY SCRIPTURES

1. "Therefore, if any man be in Christ, he is a new creature: old things are passed away; behold, all things are become new." (2 Cor 5:17)

2. "… He which hath begun a good work in you will perform it until the day of Jesus Christ…" (Philippians 1:6)

3. "Beloved, now are we the sons of God, and it doth not yet appear what we shall be: but we know that, when he shall appear, we shall be like him; for we shall see him as he is." (1 John 2:2)

4. "In my Father's house are many mansions: if it were not so, I would have told you. I go to prepare a place for you. And if I go and prepare a place for you, I will come again, and receive you unto myself; that where I am, there ye may be also." (John 14:2-3)

5. "We're Christ's representatives. God uses us to persuade men and women to drop their differences and enter into God's work of making things right between them. We're speaking for Christ himself now: Become friends with God; he's already a friend with you." (2 Corinthians 5:20)

DIVE DEEPER

1. What is the one constant in life?

2. Why does the thought of change create tension in us?

3. What are the key stages through which we must pass when we deal with change?

4. What is the ultimate motivation for change?

5. Can we become effective followers of Christ without changing?

6. What types of changes should we be making if we are trying to be like Christ?

7. What does change do to and for us as we seek to follow Jesus?

APPLICATION

1. When we strive to align ourselves with Jesus, we must realize that we have no choice but to make changes in our lives—in all aspects our lives.

2. The changes we make must have the goal of emulating the way Jesus lived and loved while He was on this earth.

3. The result of the changes we make—sanctification—will render us holy, set aside from the world, and pure in the sight of God.

4. We can look forward to a time in the future and eternity when we "shall be like Him" because we will have completely changed from sinners to saints.

AFFIRMATION

Although change can be difficult, the rewards for making the proper shifts in our lives can bring us such great rewards, both here on earth and in heaven, that only a fool would refuse to make those changes.

SUPPLICATION

Lord, I know that without changing everything in my being to align myself with Your sacred principles of life, I will be doomed. Therefore, I call upon You to cover me with Your loving grace and lead me through the adjustments I must make to become a "new creation" in Christ. Please, Lord—fill me with your Holy Spirit and change my "heart of stone" into a "heart of flesh" that can exude love and grace to all.

INVITATION

Jesus is the author of change. He is the creative essence of the universe, and He wants us to be with Him. To be with Jesus, the first thing we must do is change. Be willing to change—your behavior, your attitude, and your beliefs—if you want to be with Jesus.

MY BIBLE AND MY MINISTRY
Ministry in a Multigenerational Context

Dr. Tyrone P. Jones IV,
Senior Pastor, First Baptist Church of Guilford, Columbia, MD

Definition:

Ministry: the service, functions, or profession of a minister of religion.

Quote:

"It is not the hermeneutical skills of the preacher, or the gifts and talents, that produces the presence of Christ. The preparation and words of the proclaimer are valuable because they are means through which the encounter occurs. However, the event happens as a result of Christ, through Grace and the work of the Holy Spirit, choosing to make himself known and thus imparting strength to those who are present."
— Jerry M. Carter Jr., The Audible Sacrament:
The Sacramentality of Gardner C. Taylor's Preaching, p. 39

Scripture:

"After the death of Moses, the servant of the Lord, the Lord said to Joshua son of Nun, Moses' aide: "Moses my servant is dead. Now then, you and all these people, get ready to cross the Jordan River into the land I am about to give to them—to the Israelites. I will give you every place where you set your foot, as I promised Moses. Your territory will extend from the desert to Lebanon, and from the great river, the Euphrates—all the Hittite country—to the Mediterranean Sea in the west. No one will be able to stand against you all the days of your life. As I was with Moses, so I will be with you; I will never leave you nor forsake you." (Joshua 1:1–5)

CIRCUMSTANCE

Upon examination of the central text in Joshua 1:1-5, the prophetic interruption in the midst of mourning the death of Moses was a message that began to create an "alternate narrative" to remove the potential idolatrous nature of the "dominant narrative." This message is also a reminder that no servant of God, whomever they may be is indispensable. Though the workers of the Lord may die, the work of the Lord will never die!

It is important to note in Joshua 1 the distinctions given to the dead servant Moses and to Joshua, who is called a "minister" (or in Hebrew, a mesharet) to Moses. Joshua's role as minister was more than just an aide and because he did not perform any religious function, the title probably referred to his military function as a form of ministry assistance. The verses in Numbers 27:18-23, state that God specifically set Joshua aside to be a visible part of Moses' leadership team. Eleazar the priest laid hands on Joshua, and he was set before God and the congregation of Israel as a leader-in-waiting.

Upon Moses' death, the time had come for what God had already commissioned before the congregation of Israel: that they might not be like sheep with no shepherd to lead them. Given Joshua's spiritual vitality, the succession plan was firmly in place. But Joshua was not Moses, nor did God intend for him to be a clone of the previous leadership. Thus, it was imperative for God to reiterate his promise to Joshua and the people of Israel. As verses 3 and 4 state: "Every place that the sole of your foot shall tread upon, that have I given unto you, as I said unto Moses. From the wilderness and this Lebanon even unto the great river, the river Euphrates, all the land of the Hittites, and unto the great sea toward the going down of the sun, shall be your coast."

God further reminds Joshua of the words Moses spoke in Deuteronomy 11:24: "Every place whereon the soles of your feet shall tread shall be yours: from the wilderness and Lebanon, from the river, the river Euphrates, even unto the uttermost sea shall the coast be." These words express elements consistent with Moses that then become exclusive to Joshua. The key point of this prophetic message from God is reiterated in Joshua 1:5, when God says, "…As I was with Moses, so I will be with thee, I will not fail thee, nor forsake thee." In that verse, God encourages Joshua with an affirmation that He will be with him in presence and with power. Continuing, God says, "I will not fail thee," Confirming that God's strength will be just as powerful in Joshua's leadership of the Israelites as it was in Moses' leadership.

In verse 6, God also tells Joshua to be strong and courageous, for the arduous task of dividing the inheritance of the land among the people will fall in Joshua's lap. This parallels the final charge Moses gives to Joshua in Deuteronomy 31:23: "And he gave Joshua the son of Nun a charge, and said, Be strong and be of a good courage: for thou shalt bring the children of Israel into the land which I swore unto them: and I will be with thee." What is fascinating about God's charge is that it is given to Joshua immediately after Moses, as noted in Deuteronomy 31:19-22, had written a song at the request of the Lord and taught it to the children of Israel. The Song of Moses is a prophetic message in anticipation of future judgments to befall Israel. During the time when Moses was writing his song, Israel had done nothing to incur the wrath of God. His song, however, would later serve as a reminder of what God knew Israel was going to do in sin.

Interestingly, though God asked Moses to write and teach his song to the children of Israel, it is Joshua who is brought before the people to be Moses' successor. The very words to the song the children of Israel were forced to learn were words from a leader who was fading off the scene. The Lord encouraged Joshua to be strong and of good courage. He called for him not only to rely on the strength of God as provider of the promise but also to be courageous in his leadership of Israel. The song of Moses was a prophetic announcement of what was to come, thus Joshua had to be courageous and complete in his obedience to God. Though God called him to be a carrier of the Song of Moses, his method of executing the song was different.

As noted in Deuteronomy 34:10: "And there arose not a prophet since in Israel like unto Moses, whom the Lord knew face to face." Joshua's relationship with the Lord, although not the same as God's relationship with Moses, was just as strong. Such a "call" to ministry is indeed a distinguished and splendid calling. It is a privileged invitation to state publicly God's declaration for the plight of mankind. It compels men and women into the ministry and sustains them to execute it. As preachers, however, we must be mindful that everyone called to minister/ministry is not cut from the same mold.

The Song of Moses was placed in the mouths of the people of Israel as a prophetic annunciation of their future wiles; yet God chose Joshua to "remix" that song of rebellion with a hermeneutic of promise. At their essence, the words of a previous culture need the medium of the current culture; they also need a preacher (minister) to help articulate that hermeneutic of promise. The inspiration of Joshua and the instruction of Moses must be viewed as a prism through which God can shine the light of many different-colored perspectives, but the Gospel must be heard and remixed by courageous leaders who are ready to see the movement of God rather than be seen as the movement of God.

CONFLICT

For Christianity to be more inclusive culturally and reach further globally, the Gospel witness must be destigmatized. To truly carry out that witness faithfully, the impact of witness must not lie in the hands of the one who is witnessing. Instead, it must be carried out by the one receiving witness. As we Christians are often reminded: "Witness points away from itself."

The pre-modern period of theology was understood as an individual cognitive understanding of God and things related to God. David Bosch in his book, Transforming Mission: Paradigm Shifts in Theology of Mission, points out the following about God and things related to God: "In this sense it was habitus, a habit of the human soul…a discipline, a self-conscious scholarly enterprise."[1] Bosch details how the early enterprise of theology was individualistic and self-conscious, and how even the study of theology in its practical form was reserved for clergy only. Missions/ministries

---

[1] David J. Bosch, *Transforming Missions: Paradigm Shifts in the Theology of Mission* (Maryknoll, NY: Orbis Press, 1999), 489.

were only on the periphery of the church. Later, in the Reformed world, the practical idea of ministry as service always catered to the preservation of the institutional church. Bosch further mentions the "stigma" placed upon Third World seminaries to train native clergy to mirror and imitate the churches from the West in every way: "...the 'daughter church' had to imitate the 'mother church' in the minutest details and had to have the same structure of congregations, dioceses, clergy, and the like, it went without saying that the theology taught there would be a carbon copy of European theology."[2]

Bosch underscores the inherent danger of conceptualizing and systematizing faith without regard for true witness. Ministries designed for multiple generations for people of diverse cultural themes must possess authenticity. Within the authenticity of all ministry efforts, the God-Element should be the primary source that causes and motivates people and the foundational reason(s) people to come to know the Gospel on their own terms.

CHALLENGE

Ministry, in its orthodoxy of faith, has been negligent in its orthopraxis of love. Although the church and its witness are the only means for sharing the Gospel, it is not the church that undertakes mission—it is the *Missio Dei* (the act of sending forth) that constitutes Christian witness. Our mission then, as Christians, is not to be in competition with other religions. Our mission is not merely to engage others in the activity of conversion. It is not just about projects, politics, and economic agendas. It is to constantly be reminded of the backdrop of the *Missio Dei*, which continuously sanitizes the preacher as a individual and purifies believers' witness for the translation of the Gospel.

The minister has a responsibility to fight against the normative and reductionist display of the Gospel. The Gospel message must never be curtailed to the point where it loses its expressive form and outreach. As preachers, we must fight the effects of reducing the Gospel to being confined within a localized pastorate when God has called for it to be free within a global apostolate. The apostolate must not be pigeon-holed to the clergy, but it must be free for all to partake.

Ministers must, in the words of Henry Mitchell, "Make the biblical account into a living experience."[3] It is we who have received from God His Gospel, to be sent and to be witnessed. We must constantly be challenged as to our congregational hermeneutic. Likewise, our churches must constantly and critically look within for traces of stigmatization and normative behavior. Our witness must be constantly immersed in the Word of God and strategically positioned under the

---

[2] Ibid., 490.

[3] Henry H. Mitchell, *Celebration and Experience in Preaching*, (Abingdon Press, Nashville, TN: 1990), 87

Cross. It is through the Word of God that we Christians derive our validity, and it is under the shadow of the Cross that we maintain our humility. As we interpret the Gospel witness to people of diverse cultures, our interpretation cannot violate the translatability of God's process to make God's self known to all. As believers, we are always participants in an ongoing liberating process that has more to do with God's love through our witness for the sake of the whole world.

CHOICE

Every minister does not minister the same, but every minister shares a common denominator: to hear and obey the Voice of God. When Moses accepted the challenge to lead God's people, it was the voice of God that called him to the burning bush. Though he initially questioned his abilities to liberate an oppressed/suppressed/depressed people and believed himself inadequate to do so, Moses quickly discovered that being a leader and liberating people in the name of the Lord meant that his ministry was not about his abilities but about his availability.

Joshua was given the reigns after Moses and thus became responsible for ensuring that the children of Israel adhered to the commands of the Lord. In the current context of ministry succession, a new preacher/pastor, like Joshua, hears the voice of God, accepts what God has to say, then lifts and carries the mantle of ministry. It is very important to point out that both the Moseses (senior preacher/pastors) and the Joshuas of today are able to accept what God has to say because they both have discovered that the mission/ministry is never about who they are in light of themselves. Rather, it is about who they are in light of the One whom they serve.

As written in Exodus 3:10, God states: "Come now therefore, and I will send thee unto Pharaoh, that thou mayest bring forth my people the children of Israel out of Egypt." His decree precedes Moses' questions of deterrence when he asked God to elaborate for the people, and for himself, just who it was that Moses was chosen to represent. God clarifies this emphatically when He says to Moses, "I AM THAT I AM," and Moses subsequently affirms: "Thus shalt thou say unto the children of Israel, I AM hath sent me unto you" (Exodus 3:14, KJV). In verse 15, God sanctions these words, calling them a memorial "unto all generations."

Fast forwarding again to Joshua 1:5, the Bible confirms this need for continuous leadership and ministry, even when the new leader breaks from the one who had been leading previously. In that chapter/verse, God tells Joshua, "As I was with Moses, so I will be with thee…" This is a powerful reminder that when a minister chooses to "do" ministry, he ultimately is choosing to accept his limited role in a continuous mission that will long outlive him. Ministry, for the preacher/pastor, is perpetual, not personal.

CONSEQUENCE

Joshua accepts the mantle of Moses given to him by God and becomes part of the chain of leaders who ultimately lead the children of Israel to the Promise Land. He makes the choice to lead; yet, with every such choice both good and bad consequences can follow. The text tells us that God promises to be with him and to give him the land of his ancestors, but it is on the consequential condition that Joshua must always be "strong and courageous"—a refrain that God repeats to Joshua three times. The phrase is first encountered in Joshua 1:6: "Be strong and courageous, because you will lead these people to inherit the land, I swore to their ancestors to give them." It next appears in Joshua 1:7, when God tells Joshua, "Be strong and very courageous. Be careful to obey all the law my servant Moses gave you; do not turn from it to the right or the left, that you may be successful wherever you go." The final time, as noted in Joshua 1:9, the Lord says, "Have I not commanded you? Be strong and courageous. Do not be afraid, do not be discouraged, for the Lord your God will be with you wherever you go." In Joshua 1:7, however, God ramps up His emphasis, telling Joshua to be "strong and very courageous" when it comes to obeying His word!

In these passages, God is sharing with Joshua a key lesson for success in ministry. That lesson: to be a leader, a man must use his unique personality to solidify his position and fall in line with God's plan. God, of course, sets the plan; and it is He who places men in positions of leadership. It then is up to those leaders to ensure that their charismatic personalities adhere to God's plan. As pastors/preachers, we are called to lend our personalities to our ministry positions. We are also called to lend our personalities in our ministry positions to following God's way, wherever God leads, because God will be with us wherever we go. God is always with us, and our positions and personalities must reflect that.

God also is very particular when comes to how His leaders keep and administer the Word of God for His people to follow. A pastor/preacher's leadership, teachings, and deeds must reflect not only that he knows the Word of God, but that he is obedient to God's Word. So, I say to you, men of God and leaders in the church, do not turn to the left or to the right! To be successful in your ministries, keep the Word of God in your mouth and in your heart!

CHALLENGE

Joshua faces a huge challenge: that of living in the shadow of a great leader. As Deuteronomy 34 notes, the people of Israel greatly mourned the passing of Moses. Joshua 1:3 further maintains that God kept before Joshua the memory of Moses "as [He] promised Moses" while affirming in Joshua 1:5, "...As I was with Moses, so will I be with [Joshua]." I faced a similar challenge years ago as a new pastor. I was told that I had very big shoes to fill following my predecessor in ministry. I was unruffled in my response, however, noting confidently: "His shoes are too big for me, so I guess I will just have to walk in my own shoes." It is not uncommon, I learned, to hear the echoes of the past in the corridors of one's present ministry. The essential question regarding this challenge is:

How can the new leader use this reverence for old leadership to his advantage? As my father, the late Rev. Dr. Tyrone P. Jones III, once told me, "When you accept and acknowledge that the people you pastor had history prior to [your] coming, it makes it easier to build on the foundation that has already been laid instead of destroying what was in order to build what is not yet." The essence of what my father was sharing with me was that I had to find a way, using my position and my unique personality, to build on what was and to follow God's plan.

The mantle of leadership can be heavy and weighty at times, but those of you who are "Joshua-level" pastors/preachers must remember that God has called you precisely for such a time as this. Your time is now! Your challenge is to stand on what God gave to you and nobody else. There will be times when the people will reference the past victories and past triumphs of past leaders, but if you follow the plan and recognize your purpose, you will prevail!

Any man who picks up the mantle of leadership and ministry will have to face his own unique challenges. Moses' challenge was to lead the children of Israel out of Egypt, prepare them to cross the Red Sea, and then, for forty years, to lead them in the wilderness. When Joshua came on the scene, he had to face his own unique set of challenges. He had to lead where Moses left off and guide the people across the River Jordan to the Promised Land. Each ministry is filled with challenges, but challenges define the best of who you are and *whose* you are. Do not doubt yourself; God is priming your experiences and your personality to face whatever lies ahead of you.

CHRISTOLOGICAL PRINCIPLE

Scripture relates that Jesus Christ is the embodiment of the message, mind, and ministry of God. As stated in John 1:1: "In the beginning was the Word, and the Word was with God, and the Word was God." This passage affirms the overarching principle that Jesus Christ is the Word of God manifested among mankind. John 1:4-5 further notes that John the Baptist was a witness to the message, mind, and ministry of God (The Logos) when he states: "In Him was life, and that life was the light of all mankind. The light shines in the darkness, and the darkness has not overcome it." John 1:7 shares that Jesus came as the light and enlightenment John the Baptist preached and proclaimed to those who were in darkness (ignorance). John the Baptist was the instrument God used to magnify the message of Jesus Christ.

Just as the mantle and message was passed from Moses to Joshua, we pastors/preachers of today are positioned, for a season and a reason, to be carriers of the Gospel message and ministry of light. John came as a witness to preach about the light so that others might believe. We must never forget, however, that though we are but instruments to draw attention to the message inherit in our ministries, we were never meant to be the Messiah. We were never meant to draw the focus of our ministries toward us more so than toward Jesus Christ. As John 1:8 says, "He himself (John the Baptist) was not the light; he only came as a witness to the light."

CRISIS

In Joshua 1:1-5, the critical moment of potential crisis was not in just the passing of the prophetic mantle of ministry from Moses to Joshua; it was in Joshua's speaking in his own voice about what God had shared with him about how to take the people to the next phase of ministry. God told Joshua: "Now then, you and all these people, get ready to cross the Jordan River into the land I am about to give…" (Joshua 1:2) The difficulty in that moment was not just that Joshua was then responsible for the people. Equally as important, Joshua had to understand where he was going and how to get there. Ministry is not just about hearing from God, it is also about executing God's plan. We pastors/preachers must be clear not only in our message but also in the framework of our ministry if the people are going to follow us. We also must know the people we are to lead.

COVENANT

As stated in Joshua 1:5: "No one will be able to stand against you all the days of your life. As I was with Moses, so will I be with you; I will never leave you nor forsake you." This is a powerful spiritual covenant between the Source and the Servant, and that covenant statement is the lasting word that carries Joshua through his entire ministry. God knows the beginning from the end, so in times of uncertainty in ministry, instead of looking for a new revelation on what you should do, just remember what God shared in the beginning and tap into the source that will continue to be your supply.

CONCLUSION

Your ministry and message are not predicated on your readiness to preach or lead. They are, however, predicated on your availability and openness to be used. God does not call the qualified, but God does qualify the called!

FIVE KEY SCRIPTURES

1. "The Lord said to Moses, "Now the day of your death is near. Call Joshua and present yourselves at the tent of meeting, where I will commission him." So, Moses and Joshua came and presented themselves at the tent of meeting." (Deuteronomy 31:14)

2. "Keep this Book of the Law always on your lips; meditate on it day and night, so that you may be careful to do everything written in it. Then you will be prosperous and successful. Have I not commanded you? Be strong and courageous. Do not be afraid; do not be discouraged, for the Lord your God will be with you wherever you go." (Joshua 1:8-9)

3. "The word of the Lord came to me, saying, Before I formed you in the womb I knew[a] you, before you were born I set you apart; I appointed you as a prophet to the nations."(Jeremiah 1:4-5)

4. "Pure religion and undefiled before God and the Father is this, To visit the fatherless and widows in their affliction, and to keep himself unspotted from the world." (James 1:27)

5. "But it shall not be so among you: but whosoever will be great among you, let him be your minister; And whosoever will be chief among you, let him be your servant: Even as the Son of man came not to be ministered unto, but to minister, and to give his life a ransom for many." (Matthew 20:26-28)

DIVE DEEPER

1. What does ministry look like for the present generation? How do you craft an intergenerational message that is consistent with the historical prospective of promise while dealing with the current generational challenges of the present?

2. How does the lesson about Joshua and Moses help your ministry and your preaching? Can you relate the promises of the past to the current generation of the present?

3. How is your ministry functioning and flourishing? Is it healthy or on life-support?

4. Are your sermons stimulating the vision for the church?

5. Is your ministry ready for what's next?

6. Who (other than yourself) is championing the ministry?

7. What resources do you need to be a more effective pastor/minister?

8. When are you going to implement your ministry goals and objectives?

9. Where would it be most appropriate to make changes?

10. Is your preaching facilitating growth (spiritually and numerically) in the church? Why or why not??

APPLICATION

1. Remember you were never called to be like Moses. Your role must be relevant to the current times.

2. As a custodian of your ministry context, never forget that your position as pastor/preacher and your assignment as leader must be in tune with God's plan.

AFFIRMATION

God, I thank You for the privilege to preach to Your people and to pastor with passion! My lips of clay are Yours to command! Use my witness to work Your will!

SUPPLICATION

Dear Lord, I come to You as humble as I know how. I submit to You that I know this ministry and my purpose for preaching did not start with me and will not end with me. Thank You for my predecessors and for the ministry leaders to come who will help cultivate this community of believers. Use my current ministry efforts to advance Your Kingdom. Lord, let my will be lost in Thy Will. Amen.

INVITATION

The Lord needs laborers in the vineyard! The harvest is plentiful, but there are not enough workers for the Kingdom of God. Work while it is day, for a time is coming when men will no longer have the opportunity to work. The Lord is looking for brothers who are committed to the cause of Christ. Remember that the one who puts his hand toward the plow yet turns back is not fit for the Kingdom. The work of ministry is never easy, but God will give you strength in the struggle. In this day and time, we need brothers who are change agents for the Lord, who are willing to preach and teach the life-giving word of the Gospel. Only what you do for Christ will last!!

MY BIBLE AND MY MORALITY:

Living in a Moral Manner: Social Responsibility

Dr. Keith A. Savage,

Senior Pastor, First Baptist Church of Manassas, VA

Definition:

Morality: Behavior that conforms to justice or righteous conduct; ethical quality or character

Quote:

> *"We are what we repeatedly do. Excellence, then, is not an act but a habit."*
> — Aristotle, Greek Philosopher (circa. 384–322 BCE)

Scripture:

"You must not spread a false report. Do not join the wicked to be a malicious witness. "You must not follow a crowd in wrongdoing. Do not testify in a lawsuit and go along with a crowd to pervert justice. Do not show favoritism to a poor person in his lawsuit. "If you come across your enemy's stray ox or donkey, you must return it to him. "If you see the donkey of someone who hates you lying helpless under its load, and you want to refrain from helping it, you must help with it. "You must not deny justice to a poor person among you in his lawsuit. Stay far away from a false accusation. Do not kill the innocent and the just, because I will not justify the guilty. You must not take a bribe, for a bribe blinds the clear-sighted and corrupts the words of the righteous. You must not oppress a foreign resident; you yourselves know how it feels to be a foreigner because you were foreigners in the land of Egypt." (Exodus 23:1-9 HCSB)

CIRCUMSTANCE

Author John Ortberg, in his book, Love Beyond Reason: Moving God's Love from Your Head to Your Heart, asserts that envy is "disliking God's goodness to someone else and dismissing God's goodness to [oneself]." Ortberg goes on to define envy as "desire plus resentment" and as being "anti-community." He further describes it metaphorically as sprouting quickly from seeds of discontentment in the minds of men and growing wildly into weeds of resentment. Those weeds, he contends, can grow so close to the heart of moral human behavior that they eventually choke out God's moral standards.

For example, God expected the Israelites to live up to His moral standards, which included promoting justice rather than twisting it. Once His chosen people were settled in the Promised Land, however, they began to wallow in the ways of corruption and allow immorality and injustice to prevail. In doing so, they established a character of hypocritical worship—of simply going through the motions of worship, prayer, and other religious activities; and of envying others for the goodness God bestowed upon all equally. They planted seeds of discontent and, failing to tend the moral "soil" God gave them, they allowed the weeds of resentment to grow wild in the Promised Land.

It is perilously easy for us today to forget that God wants us to grow in our love for Him, to mature in our spiritual wisdom and understanding, and to become more like Jesus the Christ in our thoughts and actions. Biblical justice and righteousness look beyond the mere letter of the law and demand the fulfillment of responsibilities that arise out of the spirit of the law in human relationship. So how can a man eradicate envy from his heart? That process begins with developing a right attitude toward God and the blessings He bestows. A man whose life is captured by a heart incapable of exhibiting justice, mercy, and humility is too preoccupied and wayward.

Most teachings of the Bible afford little time for capturing the concerns of a faith focused on freedom and justice. Too often these truths are watered down in ways that mute any spirit of advocacy for social responsibility and God's ethic of justice; however, authenticity requires each man to pay attention to his moral role in producing practical manifestations of his witness toward social responsibility and justice. For we men particularly, Exodus 23:1-9 confirms the importance of God in our role as cultivators of lives and societies of justice, mercy, and integrity. This emphasis is stressed in Exodus 23, which proclaims that the Lord wanted His people to be holy and devoted to the purposes of God as demonstrated by living in a moral and righteous manner.

CONFLICT

Exodus 23:1. Being an Honest Person

"You must not spread a false report. Do not join the wicked to be a malicious witness."

The Bible points out that God commissioned Moses to lead the Israelites out of Egypt to the Promised Land. Even though Moses was raised in Pharaoh's house for forty years, the commitment came into his heart to no longer ignore the plight of God's people under a system of injustice. After Moses killed an Egyptian who was beating a Hebrew, he fled to Midian (Exodus 2:11-15; Acts 7:23-29). Another forty years passed, and Egypt was most likely a distant memory for Moses.

At the right moment, however, God shared with Moses the plan He had in mind all along. It was a plan that revealed God's moral stance and concern for the oppressed. God had not forgotten the children of Israel, nor had He forgotten the promises He made to their ancestors (Exodus 3:7-22; Acts 7:30-34), and justice eventually prevailed. A popular idiom speaks to this truth, which was first uttered by God: "Your word is your bond." God always keeps His promises.

For men, the starting point to understanding this lesson is learning to be honest with one another in our daily dealings, to keep our commitments, and to ensure that our word is our bond. This truth is reiterated in the New Testament, 1 John 2:5, which says, "But whoever keeps His word, truly in him the love of God is perfected." Behind such a commitment is the realization that the Lord is a God of moral truth. The ordinances recorded in Exodus 23:1-9 were intended to demonstrate the spirit in which impartial justice is to be lived out daily in the lives of men.

To help secure justice, God commanded His people to not spread baseless reports by means such as circulating malicious talk, proliferating unfounded rumors, and the like (Exodus 23:1). God further decreed that no one in the covenant community was to assist any guilty person in a scheme to bring down an innocent party. Given that many cases could be decided on the testimony of two or three witnesses, God saw the importance of forbidding false witness that could result in wrongful punishment. Learning to relate to one another in that way requires a man to no longer say the words, "Let me be honest with you," but to live a life that affirms he is always an honest man in word and deeds.

CHOICE

Exodus 23:2-3. Being a Person of Integrity

> *"You must not follow a crowd in wrongdoing. Do not testify in a lawsuit and go along with a crowd to pervert justice. Do not show favoritism to a poor person in his lawsuit."*

The book of Exodus reveals that God further instructed His people to maintain impartial justice through integrity. To have integrity is to assume individual responsibility for doing what is right according to God's word—not according to the crowd's will or a culture's opinion. Being part of a crowd is not an excuse for individual wrongdoing. As Christ Jesus warned his disciples in Matthew 7, the road that leads to destruction is wide and popular. That chapter also offers a warning against blind acceptance of testimonies and opinions that agree with the majority but pervert integrity.

As men of God, it is our responsibility to stand for what is just, even if it means standing alone. In every situation, we must seek out the truth of God's moral law. Whether rich or poor, our words and actions must uphold justice. The godly man rejects any notion or action that attempts to pervert justice by making the guilty look innocent.

Exodus 23:4-9. Living In an Upright Manner

"If you come across your enemy's stray ox or donkey, you must return it to him. If you see the donkey of someone who hates you lying helpless under its load, and you want to refrain from helping it, you must help with it."

These verses of Exodus 23 present case law on the subject of living in an upright manner. They are aimed not at the welfare of man's animals but of man's enemies. Living in an upright manner complements living in a moral manner. Upright living is based on what is right, not on what a man feels about the object or recipient of his behavior. It presumes circumstances in which a man should go out of his way to be kind to others, exhibit justice, and show compassion—even to his enemies and those who reject him.

Notice also that no penalty is attached to the case law presented in Exodus 23. Given that men's behaviors are difficult to monitor or confirm, the verses in this chapter aim more personally at the heart of man. The compassionate response to the situation posed would not be to ignore the animal of one's enemy but to stop and offer assistance. God knows that acts of compassion can help transform enemies into friends. In the New Testament, for example, Jesus instructs His disciples to love their enemies and pray for those who persecute them. This instruction is not easily followed by any of us, but it is the high calling of those who are Disciples of Christ.

Exodus 23:6-7. Being an Advocate for Justice

"You must not deny justice to the poor among you in his lawsuit. Stay far away from a false accusation. Do not kill the innocent and the just, because I will not justify the guilty."

Though the disenfranchised (the poor and oppressed) are not to be given special privileges, these verses of Exodus proclaim, neither are they to be denied justice. Rather, justice is to be the goal in every case and action, regardless of the social status of those involved. This means that more than the facts should be considered in every case and each situation must be guided by a search for the truth. A godly man, these verses maintain, will keep his distance from those who falsely accuse someone of committing a crime or immoral act. Likewise, the upright man does not support capital punishment, for capital punishment is not the point of the law. The underlying principle is justice and proper behavior toward God and with one another.

CONSEQUENCE

Exodus 23:8. Refusing to Accept a Bribe

"You must not take a bribe, for a bribe blinds the clear-sighted and corrupts the words of the righteous."

A bribe is an exchange of goods (financial or otherwise) or services in exchange for an action of illegality, dishonesty, or favoritism—for example, paying off judges, politicians, administrators, or demanding a fee just to hear a case or perform a legal right. God knew that men who engaged in the act of bribery would act greedily or discriminatorily rather than justly and, by doing so, dilute their honor, making impartial justice impossible.

The New Testament book of Acts tells us that Governor Felix held a hearing in which the Jews accused the Apostle Paul of agitation and insurrection against the Jewish faith. After hearing both sides, Felix adjourned the hearing and sent for Paul. When he arrived, Felix listened to Paul expound on his faith in Jesus Christ. The actions of Governor Felix, however, clearly nullified any intentions of impartial justice and moral behavior. As reported in Acts 24:25-26, as Paul "spoke about righteousness, self-control, and the judgment to come, Felix became afraid and replied, 'Leave for now, but when I find time, I'll call for you.' Felix was also hoping that money would be given to him by Paul. For this reason, he sent for him quite often and conversed with him." This example illustrates that part of becoming a man of morality entails living and carrying out actions that disregard the immoral and undue influence of others for a biased outcome. God's justice does not have a price tag. Men of upright living will reject bribery's temptations of personal gain and refuse to subvert social and personal justice.

CHALLENGE

Exodus 23:9. Refusing to Oppress Others

> *"You must not oppress a foreign resident; you yourselves know how it feels to be a foreigner because you were foreigners in the land of Egypt."*

The Hebrew verb for "oppress" means "to crush" and refers to actions that are abusive and overbearing. The objects of such mistreatment in the quote above are foreigners. The reason God insisted that the Israelites were to treat foreigners fairly is because the Israelites had a history of being foreigners in Egypt for nearly 450 years. His command thus was for His children to keep a personal remembrance of their roots and struggles toward justice.

A man of upright living is willing and able to show responsive empathy toward those living a present existence that connects to the upright man's past physical, emotional, or spiritual realities. Foreigners usually have no family nearby to protect them if they are attacked or abused, but God declared that foreigners deserve protection and that compassion for foreigners should have no blind spots. God knew that unless a man is willing to recognize himself in the circumstances of the oppressed and the foreigner, he will not care to protect and defend them.

CHRISTOLOGICAL PRINCIPLE

As Christ stated: "…whoever practices and teaches these commandments will be called great in the kingdom of heaven. For I tell you, unless your righteousness surpasses that of the scribes and Pharisees, you will never enter the kingdom of heaven." (Matthew 5:19b-20 HCSB). Truth has relevancy in application. Moral conduct must verify itself in practical action to our faith.

CRISIS

The injustices referred to in Exodus 23:1-9 have a modern ring to them. It parallels that of wealthy people and financial institutions in modern America. Individuals and financial institutions have gained billions of dollars unjustly while impoverishing hundreds of thousands. Do not some men experience the temptation to covet and to seek personal satisfaction at the expense of others? Focusing unfailingly on his own satisfaction leads a man to unjust actions. It crowds God out of his thinking and behavior. A man cannot love God with all his heart, soul, mind, and strength and not really be interested in what God wants from him in the realm of morality.

COVENANT

It is imperative that every man that claims to love Christ—accept the mandate to love who and what Christ loves—which is every man, every woman, and every child as well justice for all of God's children. In addition, as men who proclaim to love God, we must be willing to provide for the needy, protect the defenseless, and produce acts of charity by way of assuring justice in an unjust society. This is the charge *for and of every* man that seeks to be a son of God.

CONCLUSION

Promoting justice involves dealing and standing rightly with others and with God. Injustice grows from carelessness about others and not being interested in whether they are treated fairly. When a man cares too much for himself, he does not really care too much about anyone else. That is not living in a just or socially responsible way. Exhibiting justice and social responsibility is the true definition of a man, so live like one!

FIVE KEY SCRIPTURES

1. "The LORD of Hosts says this: Make fair decisions. Show faithful love and compassion to one another. Do not oppress the widow or the fatherless, the foreigner or the poor, and do not plot evil in your hearts against one another. (Zechariah 7:9-10)

2. "Mankind, He has told you what is good and what it is the LORD requires of you: to act justly, to love faithfulness, and to walk humbly with your God." (Micah 6:8)

3. "Wash yourselves. Cleanse yourselves. Remove your evil deeds from My sight. Stop doing evil." (Isaiah 1:16)

4. "A man's steps are established by the LORD, and He takes pleasure in his way." (Psalm 37:23)

5. "But let justice flow like water, and righteousness, like an unfailing stream." (Amos 5:24)

DIVE DEEPER

1. Discuss why it is wrong to show favoritism either to the rich or the poor?

2. How do you personally and your church collectively reach out to help the oppressed in your communities?

3. Explain how the people you associate with help or hinder your quest to be morally and socially responsible.

4. Can you relate some examples of malicious gossip you know about personally?

5. How can you resist the temptation to follow a crowd in doing what is wrong?

6. Is it or is it not proper to help those under heavy burdens (financial, physical, emotional, or spiritual)? Explain.

APPLICATION

1. When moral decisions seem difficult, remember authenticity requires attention to your moral role in producing practical manifestations of social responsibility and justice.

2. The crowd is not to be your guiding principle of righteousness, God's word is.

3. God requires you to behave properly toward God, one another, and community. This is true faith. This is true worship.

AFFIRMATION

Lord, I know you intend for my life to reflect Your moral and righteous spirit in everything I say and do.

SUPPLICATION

Lord, you have entrusted us with Your love and to exhibit moral responsibility for one another. We admit there are risks in being so loving, but selfish worry is the wrong direction. Others may be concerned about whether our upright and moral manners are worth it, but we know they are pleasing in Your sight. I pray for Your strength to never let selfish concerns prevent me from reaching out to you or to people in need. I pray my tongue will always display a confession of faith that exhibit a righteousness and justice rooted in Your will. Protect me from outside influences and crowds that would attempt to displace Your truth and justice in my opinions and decisions. I ask this and pray it all in the name of Jesus the Christ, our Lord. Amen.

INVITATION

Jesus calls you from darkness to light. It is a daily call to let the truth and root of the righteous law of God be acknowledged in what God has already done through His Son, Christ Jesus our Lord. Put your faith in God, through Christ Jesus. Faith in God is always relevant because true and purposeful living will only be received by believing God's truth about social and moral justice. It is taking God at God's Word because God's Word is God's bond!

MY BIBLE AND MY MATURITY
Grow Up!

Anthony Pappas

Definition:

Maturity: To know yourself without illusion and to act toward others with a constructive and loving spirit.

Quote:

"The measure of your maturity is how spiritual you become in the midst of your frustrations."
— Samuel Ullman

Scripture:

"Until we all attain to the unity of the faith and of the knowledge of the Son of God—a mature person, attaining to the measure of Christ's full stature." (Ephesians 4:13)

CIRCUMSTANCE

Although a description of Christ's full stature is undoubtedly beyond human comprehension, Jesus embodies four qualities to be lifted up as foundational exemplars of maturity worthy of emulation. They are 1) a healthy ego, 2) positive control of anxiety, 3) non-defensiveness, and 4) a measured response. The man who is increasingly able to incorporate these four traits into his everyday life and interactions will have gone a long way toward reflecting the maturity of Jesus Christ, our Savior, our Lord, and our Exemplar! Let us look more closely at these four qualities, how Jesus embodied them, and how we can too.

Jesus Had a Healthy Ego. The term *ego* refers to the sense of self. Every person has one, but each man must ask himself this: "Do *I* have a healthy ego, and what does a healthy sense of self look like in everyday interactions?" After his first encounter with the city council in Montgomery, Alabama, Dr. Martin Luther King Jr. realized he initially had presented his "self" to that resistant body of southern White politicians in an unhealthy manner. He had approached the council hat

85

in hand, as if asking for a favor. To achieve the goals of Montgomery's Black citizens in their mass boycott of the discriminatory city bus system, he had to embody a man with a healthy sense of self and present himself as an emerging leader in the civil rights movement—not as an inferior/slave but as an equal/citizen.

An unhealthy ego/sense of self is manifested in most men in one of two ways. Some men have developed an inferior sense of self beginning in their youth. I call such men "Mr. Milquetoast." They see themselves as inferior and act out their inferior sense of self and unhealthy egos in their everyday relationships: always deferring, never asserting, and letting others get away with more than they should.

The other extreme I call the "Big Man Syndrome" or BMS. This refers to a man who, as Paul rightly warns us against in Romans 12:3, "thinks more highly of himself than he ought." BMS is a tricky thing, however. All men are created by God and within every man is the echo of God's divine creation and the impulse to recognize this spark of God. Yet, when we men elevate our sense of importance and significance beyond our God-given "creaturely-ness," BMS has struck. When we strut and brag and puff ourselves up, our egos have definitely become unhealthy.

If any man had a rightful claim to BMS, it was Jesus. Born of the Spirit, announced as God's Son by the heavenly voice, capable of miraculous actions, Jesus remains the biggest man I know! Yet when Jesus walked among us, He did not embody a Big Man's sense of self. His sense of self included not only his identity as God's son but also His identity as a servant leader. Jesus did not take his service role to the point of servility, however. He was not cowered by power. He argued with false teachers and stood up to the Romans. No one could ever call Jesus "Mr. Milquetoast"! No, Jesus exhibited a healthy ego, avoiding the extremes of having an overly important sense of self on the one hand or a devaluated one on the other!

Jesus Exercised Positive Control Over Anxiety. What is anxiety? Whereas fear typically is a response to harm or possibility of harm that can be specified and addressed, anxiety is a generalized sense of ill, threat, or danger. Anxiety is almost a state of being; a basic worry that obscures fundamental elements of trust. Given its diffuse nature, anxiety is very difficult to address.

Jesus no doubt experienced anxiety, but it did not control his behavior. Instead, He channeled his anxiety into growth and obedience. Luke 9:51, for example, relates that Jesus "set his face" to Jerusalem knowing full well that death was in store for Him, yet He kept on course. Upon arriving in Gethsemane, though He sweated blood, Jesus stayed true to his calling and mission. Later, in Luke 12:22-28, Jesus instructs us to "be not anxious," specifically not about food and clothing, noting how God cares for the birds and the plants.

Jesus feels the need to instruct us to control our anxieties indicates just how strongly present anxiety is in our lives. For many, anxiety is the controlling force of their existence and exerts its corrosive influence in at least two ways: either to debilitate us or to drive us to respond inappropriately. In the former way, anxiety can make us so concerned about negative outcomes that we become hesitant to act and, in our failure to take action, allow the negative consequences we were anxious about to come to fruition! In the latter, anxiety can paralyze and prevent us from taking the steps that our minds or the Bible invite us to take. Anxiety can also drive us to overreact, to say and do things that are grossly out of proportion to our situation. To counter anxiety, Jesus promises us peace, first with God and subsequently with and within ourselves.

The question is: can you avail yourself to this gift of our Lord?

Jesus Exhibited Non-Defensiveness. The emotional state of defensiveness occurs when we feel threatened or under attack. In such situations, we often seek to defend ourselves by justifying our actions or stance or by counterattacking. Yet, even in the face of specific encounters—for example, when being grilled by a group of antagonists (Matthew 22: 15-22), Jesus answered them so well and so calmly. They were simply left in a state of amazement.

Similarly, we Christians can move beyond defensiveness by incorporating deeply into our souls two fundamental truths. The first is that we each are sinners saved by God's grace. Thus, when our failures, shortcomings, or sins are thrown in our faces, we always have the option of saying, "Yes, I was wrong, but I am forgiven!" Additionally, because we believe that God's love is eternal and beyond contradiction, we know, as attested in Romans 8:38-39, that nothing can separate us from the love of God. We are eternally secure in God's love, so no earthly threat can cause us any lasting harm. Furthermore, defensive reactions rob us of opportunities to learn and grow. When somebody points out your failures or shortcomings, they actually are offering you a chance to rectify your actions and change your behavioral repertoire. It takes a real man to say, "Thanks for pointing that out. I will make good and make sure I do not do that again."

Jesus Offered Measured Responses to Threats. In John 18:37, the Bible says that when Jesus was dragged before Pilate, he "answered not a word," and when he finally did respond, it was not with anxiety or defensiveness but with a statement of his identity and spiritual reality.

Too often we respond in immature ways because we respond too quickly. We let anxiety or defensiveness or a pattern of arrogance or false humility take control of our behavior. As a result, we often blurt out harsh words or snide comments or swing our fists before our minds have a chance to assess the situation at hand. Ironically, we humans are biologically programmed to do exactly that! A part of our brain is actually "wired" to short circuit rational thought in threatening circumstances, thus causing us to act irrationally in ways we often come to regret. The old adage that exhorts an angered person to count to ten before responding to a perceived danger or affront is actually a very helpful admonition. Mature men build into their responses a moment to reflect before taking action—be it to ignore or retaliate against a threat. Counting to ten can be one of the most Christ-like things we can do!

CONFLICT

Conflict would be much less a problem if we men matured spiritually as quickly as we mature physically. Personal and spiritual maturation is not so easily attained, however. It is difficult, slow, and painful. In short, it is work! None of us really wants to grow up, nor do we want to pay the price of gaining maturity or want to admit that we need to change, grow, and develop. That is hard work! No, we tell ourselves, we like ourselves just the way we are (even though most others have a different assessment of us).

For a man to acknowledge his need to grow up is to admit that he is deficient, that he fails to meet the expectations God has of him. That is not a comfortable feeling. So, men engage in internal conflict, avoid or fail to endure the pain of self-actualization, and lose the will to grow spiritually and morally. Every man is conflicted when faced with this choice.

CHOICE

The good news, as related in the Bible, is that growing up is a decision we men can and must make. It is our God-given choice. But we are not passive recipients of maturity—no, it doesn't work that way, and it is not that easy. We first must place ourselves in the hands of the Divine Potter and allow Him to reshape us in the direction of the full maturity of Jesus our Lord and Savior. God does not desire men to remain selfish and self-centered.

Joshua 24:15 admonishes men to "Choose you this day whom you will serve." If you choose God, then He expects you to become a responsible being. Put away your childish and foolish behaviors and mature in His word!

CONSEQUENCE

Admit it: if we Christians were actually fully mature; the Gospel would be more compellingly attractive to nonbelievers. Someone once observed that the reason more folks do not enter through the door of salvation is that so many Christians are clogging it up by not moving forward! We eagerly accept the salvation offered by Jesus but refuse to follow Jesus onward to our highest personal and spiritual maturity. Certainly, we could all be better evangelists and share the good news of Christianity more frequently, but the critical failing is that we good-news sharers do not exhibit sufficient spiritual growth to entice nonbelievers to follow the Jesus Way.

CHALLENGE

Can we, as men of God, commit ourselves to choose maturity consistently? Can we understand maturity as a process and work at it, in season and out? Are we willing to admit that we are not perfect (or anywhere close!) and accept the Holy Spirit's work on our spirits? We all must admit one truth: that it is not easy laying aside all the weights that so easily beset us (Hebrews 12:1). Nevertheless, as men of faith we must allow the wisdom of God to infuse our hearts for the sole purpose of maturing us in spirit as we seek to discover and walk in the fullness of our divine purpose.

CHRISTOLOGICAL PRINCIPLE

Ephesians 4:13 encourages us to "attain the measure of Christ's full stature."

Jesus provides us with the model, the pattern, and the content of personal and spiritual maturity.

CRISIS

Families, congregations, and the entire Kingdom of God all are impacted by your choice to mature or not! The very witness to the Lordship of Jesus Christ depends, in some measure, on whether you are growing into Christ's likeness or just playing spiritual games and mouthing "Jesus, Jesus," but your heart is far from God. Though this may be a personal, individual decision, it is also so much more than that. It is a testimony as to whether Jesus is the Lord, we Christians claim Him to be and whether we can demonstrate that Christ can change others' lives because He has changed ours!

COVENANT

Will you, with God, and a small group of trusted fellow Christian men, encourage each other's forward progress? Will you form an accountability group to help you monitor your own and your brothers' progress and keep each of you laser-focused on attaining the fullness of Christ? Will you willingly sign a covenant with them to achieve those ends? Will you choose to grow up?

CONCLUSION

We each are born immature. The spiritual quest of life, however, is to mature. Obviously, a newborn boychild is only a small fraction of the size and weight he will become when fully grown. What is not always quite so obvious is that God has designed the same process to operate in our psyches and spirits. We are born to grow up internally as well as externally.

When babies are hungry, thirsty, or uncomfortable, they will cry and fuss until their needs are met. This is an acceptable strategy for babies because they do not know any better, nor do they have the capacity to behave differently. This is not acceptable practice for grown men, who are expected to exhibit self-control and to be considerate of the needs of others. Nevertheless, scripture alerts us that God expects men to grow in the admonition of God's will and to reflect Him as our Lord and Savior in our lives. It is therefore the responsibility of all Christian men to grow up and play a pivotal role in the lives of those who also seek to serve God. Whenever men display Christian maturity, within and outside their homes, surely others will attempt to emulate and imitate them in their roles as servants of God.

FIVE KEY SCRIPTURES

1. "And Jesus increased in wisdom and stature, and in favour with God and man." (Luke 2:52)

2. "But Jesus held his peace, And the high priest answered and said unto him, I adjure thee by the living God, that thou tell us whether thou be the Christ, the Son of God." (Matthew 26:63)

3. "Let no corrupt communication proceed out of your mouth, but that which is good to the use of edifying, that it may minister grace unto the hearers." (Ephesians 4:9)

4. "If any of you lack wisdom, let him ask of God, that giveth to all men liberally, and upbraideth not; and it shall be given him. But let him ask in faith, nothing wavering. For he that wavereth is like a wave of the sea driven with the wind and tossed. (James 1:5-6)

5. "When I was a child, I spake as a child, I understood as a child, I thought as a child: but when I became a man, I put away childish things." (1 Corinthians 13:11)

DIVE DEEPER

1. Name a time when you felt led to interject yourself in a situation in which you observed someone being mistreated?

2. Share an incident when you felt compelled by God to involve yourself in a matter that included you or a family member?

3. Recall a moment when you didn't get involved in a friend's quarrel and it landed him/her in jail?

4. Revisit a moment that you still regret not speaking out for someone less fortunate than yourself.

5. Have you ever felt the prodding of God in your life—to be—to do—to say—or to go?

6. Can you remember a time a woman in your life suggested that you simply, "Grow up!?

APPLICATION

1. Write out three of your favorite scriptures and share them with someone.

2. Write out ten of your favorite scriptures and make an agreement with yourself to commit them to memory within the next thirty days.

3. Send a distant friend a copy of your ten favorite scriptures by mail and not by an email.

AFFIRMATION

Whenever man is ready to learn—God is ready to teach. Whenever a man sows his time into the word of God—that word will definitely grow within that man and people around him will notice the difference.

SUPPLICATION

It is my prayer for every man who reads this essay that God blesses you to mature in a manner that exceeds every and all expectations of yourself and your loved ones. May the maturity of God's love rest, rule, and abide upon you—now and forevermore.

INVITATION

I solicit you to invite God into some of the most challenging areas of your life. I encourage you to allow your pain to be the canvass of God's might and power. I beseech you to allow God to handle the items that you have been carrying for too long. Let go and let God help you grow into the man that He wants you to become.

MY BIBLE AND MY MIND:
Living the Christian Life to its Fullest

Gerald Lamont Thomas, Ph.D.,
Senior Pastor Emeritus, Shiloh Baptist Church, Plainfield NJ

Definition:

Mind: The seat of thinking, reflection and consciousness, comprising the faculties of perception and understanding; it implies moral interest and not mere unreasoning opinion.

Quote:

> *"A mind is a terrible thing to waste."*
> — United Negro College Fund

Scripture:

"Let this mind be in you which was also in Christ Jesus." — Philippians 2:5

CIRCUMSTANCE

In observing the immediate conditions of the world at large, it is apparent to anyone with a critical eye to conclude that the planet on which we live is in serious trouble, day in and day out. Modern culture presents an apparent affront to Christendom. Either people today are not thinking, or they have become heartless. Confronted with crises from every direction—from global military crises to international corruption, ecological disasters to worldwide pandemics, bipartisan politics to human trafficking—church leaders of today must rethink their position within the Body of Christ.

These myriad disastrous conditions puzzle the psyches of those of us who want a better life and who believe that our faith in Christ assures us such blessings. One scripture that readily comes to mind in considering these matters, however, is Proverbs 23:7a: "For as one thinks in her/his heart, so is s/he." Those who seriously stand on the Word of God envision having life and having it more abundantly.

Scholars generally have come to believe that the will of humanity is centered within the brain and how it functions socially, morally, intellectually, and spiritually. As Harry Blamires, in his classic book, *The Christian Mind*, asserts: "In the Christian moral system the key sin is pride—that perversion of the will by which the self is asserted as the center of the universe. That is the mark of the utterly lost soul; an established and constant habit of manipulating all people and all interests in the service of the self." The key resolution to avoid becoming a pawn in the systemic evils of Satan's world is to receive the love, grace, and mercy of the Son of God, Jesus Christ, as one's personal Lord and Savior.

Jesus clearly understood his earthly mission to redeem and restore a fallen humanity and to guide humankind toward establishing and maintaining a right relationship with His Father, the Almighty God. The Bible teaches through the words of Jesus, who said: "For I did not come to call the righteous, but sinners to repentance" (Matthew 9:13) and "For the Son of Man is come to seek and to save that which was lost." (Luke 19:10) The hallmark of having a personal relationship with Jesus is realizing that one can have salvation, peace, and blessings on Earth while being assured of eternal life with the Father in heaven. No longer must the utterly lost soul remain condemned and destitute to eternal damnation, for Jesus, "who knew no sin became sin" for all humanity, for all time, and was "a ransom for many." Thus, the process of becoming like the Master/Rabbi/Teacher is a mandate and requirement for living life to its fullest.

CONFLICT

The problematic nature of the human mindset derives from God's willingness to give individuals the opportunity to have free will, existential abilities, and personal desires. Throughout the course of biblical history, human beings have never been pigeonholed or hammer locked into a must-do, singular path of reasoning or lifestyle. After the fall of Adam and Eve in the Garden of Eden, the resulting state of no longer being sin free changed the thought processes of humankind forever. The battle for the human mind has persisted since Adam and Eve's disobedience, and it continues to permeate the cultural standards of church leaders and parishioners alike.

The Apostle Paul—a converted murderer, executioner, and persecutor of Christians—addressed this tendency toward sinful thinking before he met Christ on the Damascus Road. As he wrote in his introductory statements to the Church of Corinth:

> *"Now we have received not the spirit of the world, but the spirit which is of God; that we might know the things that are freely given to us of God. Which things also we speak, not in the words which man's wisdom teaches, but which the Holy Ghost teaches, comparing spiritual things with spiritual. But the natural man receives not the things of the Spirit of God; for they are foolishness unto him; neither can he know them, because they are spiritually discerned. For who has known*

the mind of the Lord, that he may instruct him? But we have the mind of Christ." (1 Corinthians 2: 12-14, 16)

Paul emphatically warns this body of believers that without the Spirit of God, the natural man is unspiritual (without God) and denied any opportunity of knowing God's will.

The struggles between good and evil, light and darkness, right and wrong, morality and immorality, flesh and spirit, sinner and saved, heaven and hell are all vividly portrayed within the thinking of everyone's mind. For example, I can recall on several occasions while living in my parents' home that my mischievous devilment caused my mother to scream, "Boy, have you lost your mind?!" Is it realistic to believe, however, that one can lose something that has been endowed to them by God? In Luke 15:17, when the Prodigal Son "came to himself" after his multiple bizarre escapades, was his right spiritual mind restored unto him? Fortunately, Christians do not ascribe to the view that "once a sinner, always a sinner." Instead, we hold that all believers are blessed to have the mind of Christ.

CHOICE

Armed with a clearer understanding of the spiritual make up of humankind, we can turn now to both the benefits and the disasters of making choices—either rational or irrational—for living a life that glorifies God. Blamires, who does not write from a Christian perspective, defines the thinking mind within the spheres of two categories: secular and Christian. Regarding the former, he posits: "…to think secularly is to think within a frame of reference bounded by the limits of our life on earth; it is to keep one's calculations rooted in this-worldly criteria."

Thus, secular beings participate in living the worldly life of selfish, greedy individualism. Using this frame of reference, one never calculates the negative effects of making wrong decisions or ill-advised choices based upon the limited view of living in the moment. If all one thinks will ever happen to him or her ends at the grave, then humanity lacks the eternal reality check of heaven and life everlasting. Therefore, the compass for one's choices, and one's ability to comprehend options designated for the common good, are beyond one's spiritual landscape.

The privilege of living life beyond one's own personal lens and trusting in the redeeming acts of Jesus Christ makes salvation more than just a theological presupposition. As Blamires goes on to say: "to think christianly is to accept all things with the mind as related, directly or indirectly, to man's eternal destiny as the redeemed and chosen child of God." If one desires to follow Christ and His doctrine, then one must choose to pick up their individual "cross" or spiritual burden and follow Him.

Such a decision is the final consummation and coronation of the regeneration process, thereby affirming the words of the great hymn: "I Have Decided to Follow Jesus—no turning back, no turning back." Once a person makes a conscious decision to live for the Son of God, they are then obligated to adhere to the commandments of Jesus, in which He profoundly states: "Love the Lord your God with all your heart and with all your soul and with all your mind and with all your strength; You shall love your neighbor as yourself." (Mark 12:30-31) Therein lies real essence of knowing (by faith) what options are available and mandated for the Christian mind.

CONSEQUENCE

It seems very difficult at times for Christian thinkers to distinguish between choosing between their mental capacity and their moral condition. Whether one chooses to remain in obedience to the God who creates and sustains all things or become defiant and disobedient cleaving to personal desires and demonic temptations, everyone faces consequences. The redeemed of the Lord are always in spiritual warfare, given the battle between the spiritual mind and the carnal mind.

The Apostle Paul wrestles with this inner conflict in his writings to the Church at Rome. As he notes: "I find then a law, that when I would do good, evil is present within me. For I delight in the law of God after the inward man; but I see another law in my members, warring against the law of my mind, and bringing me into captivity to the law of sin which is in my members." (Romans 7:21-23) Natural persons are sinful from birth and thereby must recognize a need to find hope and help to overcome their physical inclination to sin. The most severe consequence is described in Romans 6:23, which states: "For the wages of sin is death." Such a separation surely will be experienced spiritually, physically, emotionally, psychologically, socially, and, in the end, tragically and eternally.

If one thinks worldly thoughts, creates flesh-based attitudes, performs negative behaviors, devises evil viewpoints, and maintains wrong perspectives, one definitely cannot walk in the Spirit. As noted in Romans 8:5b: "Those who are according to the Spirit and are controlled by the desires of the Spirit set their minds on and seek those things which gratify the Spirit." The mind must be constantly renewed through a spiritual metamorphosis that denounces worldliness on every level and attains the required transformation through a blood transfusion that represents Calvary.

Another formidable effect of being without a spiritual, moral, or sanctified mindset hinges upon denial that Jesus is Lord and refusal to relinquish personal passions so as to follow Christ. In Luke 9:26, Jesus emphatically declared that "the penalty of being ashamed of him will result in him being ashamed of you before God and His witnesses in glory." Being out of Christ-like character or devoid of a Christian mentality at the judgment seat will negate the Lord's voice from saying "Well done, thy good and faithful servant," which ultimately means that one will be denied entrance into glory.

CHALLENGE

The primary problem circumventing one's receptiveness to "letting this mind be in you" formulates within the dimensions of a believer being spiritual and natural simultaneously. For there is always warring within man because of the multi-dimensional reality of man (mental, spiritual and physical. This paradox seemingly keeps one out of balance and struggling to gain enlightenment, often in a state of abnormality due to existing as a tripartite being.

The desire to live a Godly, holy life and seek the Kingdom of God and His righteousness is a consistent threat to the devil's plot and plan to kill, steal, and destroy our destiny. To be like Christ, one must possess the mind of Christ. Another key factor within this struggle is the need to remove doubt, fears, confusion, anxiety, judgment, and passivity from one's mind. As the prophet states in Isaiah 26:3, God's heavenly promise is that He will keep "in perfect peace [one] whose mind is stayed" on Him.

The final analysis of this quasi-theological matter involves realizing that one can have the mind of Jesus, the only individual who ever lived on earth without sin. Yet, how does the born-again experience bring one into a right perspective of accepting God's plan for learning how to discern between life and death? In the book, *Battlefield of the Mind: Winning the Battle in Your Mind,* Joyce Meyer offers seven practical steps for maintaining the mind of Christ: 1) think positive thoughts; 2) be God-minded; 3) be "God-Loves-Me"-Minded; 4) have an exhortative mind; 5) develop a thankful mind; 6) be Word-minded; and 7) be meditative-minded.

CHRISTOLOGICAL PRINCIPLE

Several practical teachings apply to the principles of the Christian mind. If people were to imagine, for example, what their lives might be like upon adopting the attitude of the Son of God, I believe they would find their living to operate in the realms of 1) priorities, 2) passion and 3) personality. Given that priorities drive actions, passion governs decisions, and personality creates behavior, living life to the fullest in the Christian mindset would result in major changes readily visible to others. As the Bible teaches, "…therefore, if any person is in Christ, they are new creations—old things are passed away; behold, all things are become new." (I Cor. 5:17)

During my early discipleship training at the Mount Zion Missionary Baptist Church in Los Angeles, where Dr. E. V. Hill was the esteemed pastor for over forty years, I studied a lesson in a class facilitated by Deacon Everett Woods entitled "What is the Difference?" The class focused on how to distinguish the difference in a person's life after that person has been born again and has accepted Jesus Christ as their personal Lord and Savior. As Deacon Woods explained, Christians know they are saved because the Bible teaches salvation (John 3:16). Likewise, Christians can testify that their sins are forgiven because forgiveness is in the Word of God (I John 1:9). There is power in the believer's life because Jesus promised to send it in the person of the Holy Spirit (Acts 1:8).

Thinking and acting like Jesus are natural realizations that emerge from the relationship He has with the Father. With Jesus fully in control, one's personality, temperament, and disposition will become aligned with His. In essence, it is all about being transformed by the renewing of your mind. God really does love us just the way we are, like how He loves His only begotten Son, but the Father refuses to leave us that way. The power of God's redemption seeks to place us in perfect harmony with the Son and Holy Spirit. Thus, the Father cleanses us of our filthiness, immorality, prejudice, greed, anger, dishonesty, lying tongues, and bitterness. He offers us the best opportunity to be like His Son, Jesus Christ.

It is unimaginable to have the mind of Christ and then become unlike Christ. Yet, to live the born-again life, one also must have a new heart to merge with that new mind. The heart, according to biblical theology, is the seat of human will and understanding. For example, David asked the Lord "to create in [him] a clean heart O God and renew in [him] a right spirit" (Psalms 51:10). The heart of the Master, as noted in Luke 19:10, was pure—without sin, spot or blemish, and peaceable—under Spiritual control, never seeking revenge and always forgiving; and purposeful—mission-minded "to seek and to save the lost." Jesus was led by an unseen hand. He was submitted to the Father and empowered by the Spirit. The same Spirit that created intimacy with the Father for the Son was not the result of a last resort, but a first response.

CRISIS

To live for Jesus, one must develop spiritually and learn how to think like Jesus. The crisis in today's secular culture is within the mindset of generations X, Y and Z. I am convinced that hip hop/rap music, social media, and the drug culture all have played into the hands of satanic thinking and demonic devices. This is evident in the gun violence that is on the rise daily and the rising number of communities seeking to become apothecaries for new drug-taxation schemes. More prisons are being built than educational facilities. The future looks bleak. We've allowed the village to withdraw from its responsibility and family values to fall deep within the cracks and crevices of "name it, claim it, and blame it."

How much of human failure can be attributed to the Church for not being a prominent spiritual voice in the village marketplace? Who really knows what the Christian mind is thinking if it only seeks to have utterance within the sacred Church? Why won't those who know the truth, speak the truth in love—for the betterment of social order and the well-being of the least of these? If political leaders believe in establishing a government for the people and by the people, then why do its citizens vote and promote principles of corporate privilege for the rich and greedy and constantly neglect the cries and concerns of the poor and needy? As we look around us and see the turbulent, tumultuous situations within other nations and our own, we know that these multiple crises could lead to revolution. Then what? This reality of our current times could be the rub that allows the biblical text to become the critical context for individual transformation and personal achievement.

COVENANT

As Paul writes in Philippian 2:5, "Let this mind be in you, which was also in Christ Jesus." From that vantage point, there must be a desire on the part of the individual—whether convert or disciple—to want the mind of Jesus Christ. The "mind" that Paul mentions, however, must be one that is willing to care for others by avoiding selfish ambitions. One cannot get the mind if one is not willing to do the work by humbly serving others beyond oneself. Therefore, the contractual covenant is not just between the Christian and Christ, but between the Christian, Christ, and the multitudes standing in need of loving kindness and tender mercies.

CONCLUSION

1. Human nature consists of a mind in need of regeneration.

2. God has provided the remedy for sinful persons to have a transformed mind.

3. Belief in Jesus Christ, the Son of God, is the only means whereby a sinner can be saved and have the correct relationship with God, the Father, to receive the mind of Christ.

4. Satan desires to prevent persons from obtaining the mind of Christ because therein lies the power and the will to become liberated from worldliness, pride, and selfishness.

5. One must take vital and necessary measures to maintain the mind of Christ.

6. To live a Christian life to its fullest, a believer must always have the mind of Christ.

FIVE KEY SCRIPTURES

1. "Love the Lord your God with all heart and with all your soul and with all your mind and with all your strength." (Mark 12:30)

2. "But seek ye first the Kingdom of God and His righteousness; and all these things shall be added unto you." (Matthew 6:33)

3. "I beseech you therefore, brethren, by the mercies of God, that you present your bodies a living sacrifice, holy, acceptable unto God, which is your reasonable service. And be not

conformed to this world: but be ye transformed by the renewing of your mind, that you may prove what is that good, and acceptable, and perfect, will of God." (Romans 12:1-2)

4. "Let this mind be in you which was also in Christ Jesus." (Philippians 2:5)

5. "Thou will keep him in perfect peace, whose mind is stayed on thee; because he trusts in thee." (Isaiah 26:3)

DIVE DEEPER

1. Why is having a Christian Mind mandatory in African American Church culture?

2. Why do young people between the ages of twelve and eighteen need to develop a personal relationship with Jesus Christ as their Lord and Savior?

3. How can believers in Christ overcome the conflict between the natural mind and the spiritual mind?

4. Explain how you may have suffered tragedy personally by not having the mind of Christ.

5. Is it necessary to put others before yourself to do the will of the Lord? Why/Why not?

6. What concerns do you have when it comes to taking a stand for Christ in the midst of other individuals who think with a secular, natural, or worldly mind?

7. Can a double-minded person please the Lord? Why/Why not?

APPLICATION

God gave us minds to be utilized for His glory and honor. With the fall of humanity, Satan wants us to use our minds for selfish gains and to fulfill our personal desires. To overcome our sinful nature, Jesus took on human flesh to serve as our mediator and to save our souls from eternal damnation.

1. The minds of those who place their hope and trust in the blood, death, and resurrection power of Jesus Christ will always be at war. To gain victory over this life, Christians must surrender to the will of God, seek first the Kingdom, and sacrifice themselves for others in society who need their love and assistance.

2. Trust the Word of God as the means and method for achieving life's highest degree of spiritual satisfaction. The mind of Christ will enable and empower a believer to reach their maximum potential in this life and ultimately be rewarded for their devotion in the next life.

AFFIRMATION

I will possess the mind of Christ because this is God's will for my life.

SUPPLICATION

Every day is a blessing from the Lord. Lord, please grant me the strength and power to become the Christian person I am destined to be. I struggle constantly with the many distractions and sinful desires that seek my attention and my faith. Grant me the mind of Christ, who died that I might live for His glorious honor. In turn, I will be a blessing to those who are struggling to find their way. May godliness, servanthood, humility, sacrifice, and worship become my personal goals to fulfill my purpose in the Kingdom.

INVITATION

The saints of old sang a song entitled "I Woke Up This Morning with My Mind Stayed on Jesus." Our parents sang it during the Civil Rights Movement. There is no harm in keeping your mind stayed on Jesus, singing, and praying with your mind stayed on Jesus. We need the mind of Christ. Given that Jesus is the keeper and the restorer of the human mind, ask Him today to forgive your sins, to come into your heart, and to set your mind on the heavenly things above. Ask Him to become your personal Lord and Savior. If you call, He will answer.